THE
COMPLETE
GUIDE TO
HORSE &
PONY CARE

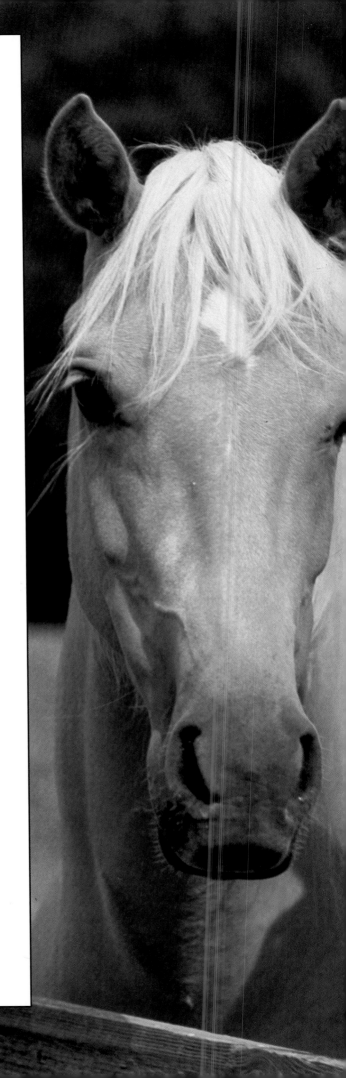

Stanley Paul & Co. Ltd
An imprint of the Random Century Group
20 Vauxhall Bridge Road, London SW1V 2SA

Random Century Australia (Pty) Ltd
20 Alfred Street, Milsons Point, Sydney, NSW 2061

Random Century New Zealand Limited
191 Archers Road, PO Box 40-086, Glenfield,
Auckland 10

Century Hutchinson South Africa (Pty) Ltd
PO Box 337, Bergvlei 2012, South Africa

First published 1991

Set in 11/12 pt Century Schoolbook
by Print Origination Ltd, Aldershot

Printed and bound in the People's Republic of China

A catalogue record for this book is available
upon request from the British Library.

ISBN 0 09 175059 8

THE COMPLETE GUIDE TO HORSE & PONY CARE

Consultant Editor
JANE KIDD

Contents

1 Basic biology

Points of a horse

Each part of the horse has a different name – called a 'point'. Knowing the points of the horse is the first stage in learning about conformation (shape) and is the basis of recognizing a good or bad horse.

When learning to ride, your instructor often refers to the different parts of the horse so it's important to memorize the correct names as soon as possible. It's also useful to know the names whenever you want to describe any affected areas to a vet.

The most important points are shown below and those most often talked about are printed in capital letters.

⭐ **MEASURING A HORSE**

Horses are measured in 'hands' — one hand is 4in (about 10cm). When a horse is not an exact number of hands high, the inches in between are shown by a point. For example, a pony which measures 12 hands and 2 inches is said to be 12.2 hands high.

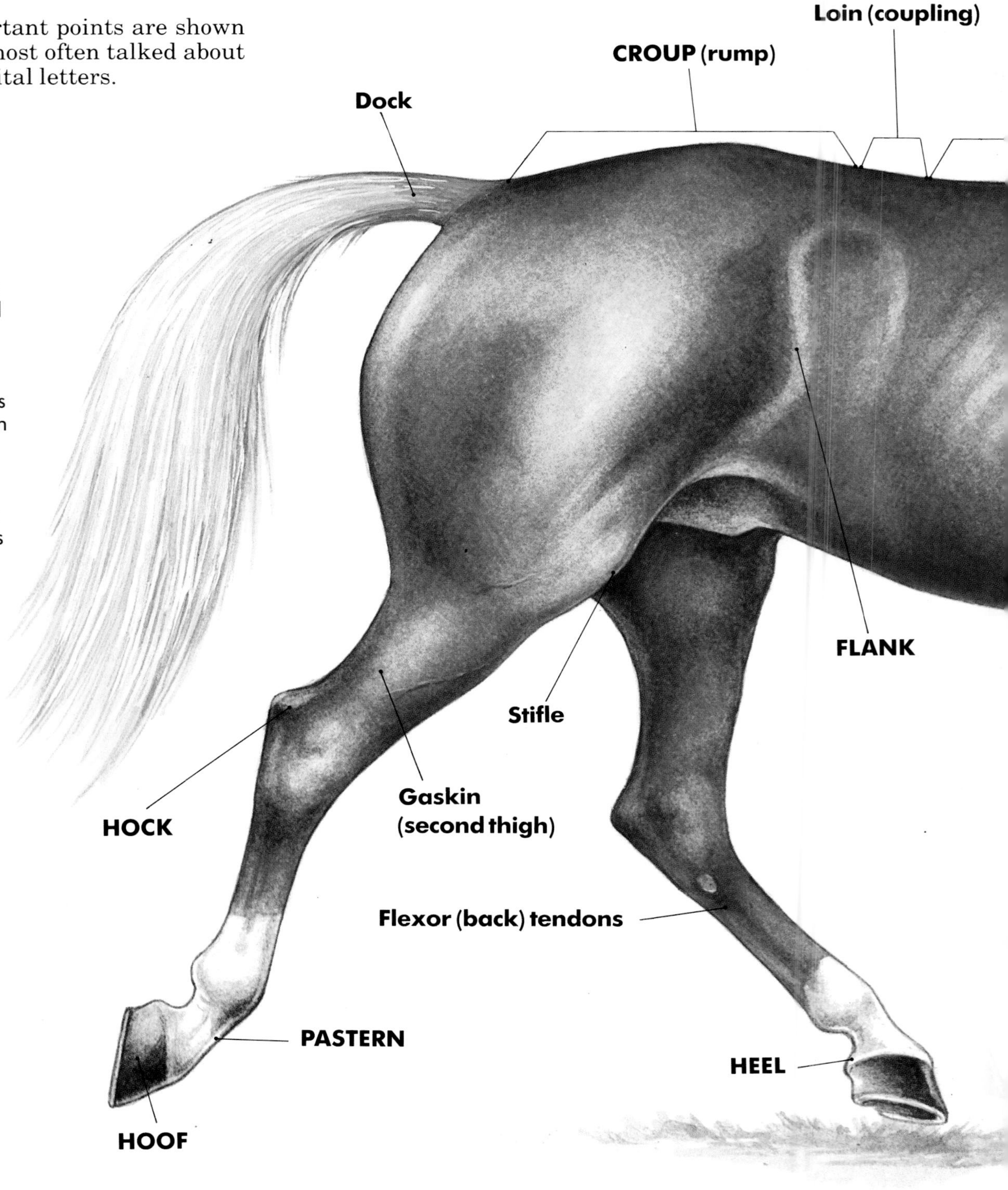

Loin (coupling)

CROUP (rump)

Dock

FLANK

Stifle

HOCK

Gaskin (second thigh)

Flexor (back) tendons

PASTERN

HEEL

HOOF

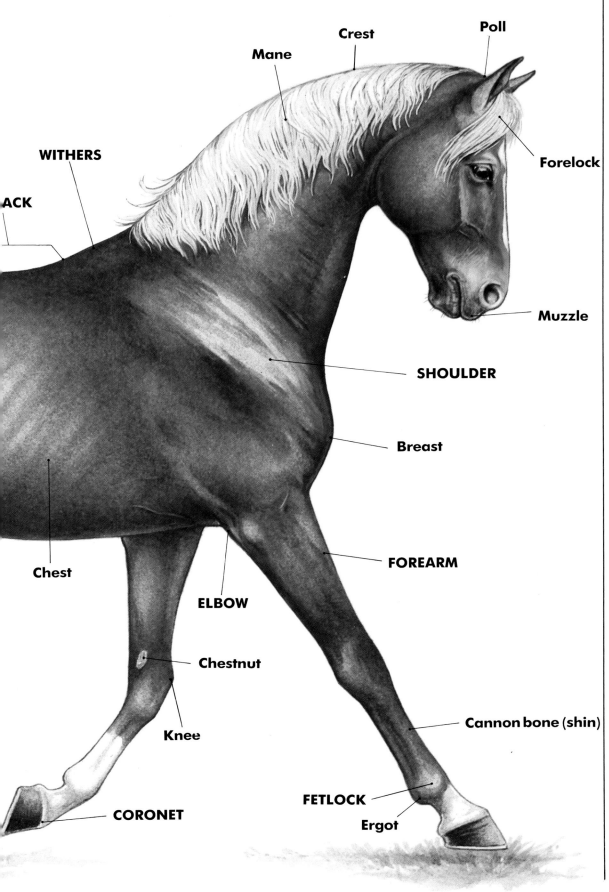

Crest

Mane

Poll

Forelock

WITHERS

ACK

Muzzle

SHOULDER

Breast

FOREARM

Chest

ELBOW

Chestnut

Knee

Cannon bone (shin)

CORONET

FETLOCK

Ergot

★ HIGHEST
POINTS
Apart from the ears,
the **poll** is the horse's
highest point when it is
standing upright.
But, because horses
have a tendency to
toss their heads about,
a horse's height is
measured from the
withers to the ground.
From a side or back
view, the **croup**
(rump) is the highest
point of the
hindquarters.

DID YOU KNOW?
The horse's four
chestnuts (the
growths about
halfway down the
inside of the leg) are
as individual to him as
our fingerprints are to
us. Because of this,
colour photographs
of a horse's chestnuts
make useful clues for
identifying stolen
animals.

9

Conformation 1: front/back

Front view

When viewed from in front, an imaginary line drawn from the point of the horse's shoulder should pass through the centre of his knee, fetlock and foot. The distance between the imaginary lines down each limb should stay the same from the chest to the feet.

Conformation means a pony's make and shape — the features he has inherited from his parents, the characteristics of his type or breed and the individual appearance that makes him unique.

What can go wrong?

Very few horses possess perfectly shaped legs. Most horses are sound with minor blemishes, which would only mark them down in the showing ring and are not important athletically. But there are some defects which make a pony more prone to lameness.

Often these faults are due to uneven distribution of the horse's weight down his leg. The legs should be straight — if the limb bends inward or outward, extra pressure is placed on some parts. This can lead to injury and causes uneven wear of hooves or shoes.

Forelegs

There are a number of defects that put strain on the legs and affect movement.

Bench knees: The cannon bones are offset outward below the knee. This can cause splints.

Knock knees: The limbs bend inward at the knee. This puts strain on the ligaments.

Knees

Bench knees

Knock knees

Foreleg defects

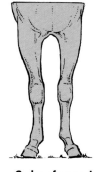

Splay footed

Pigeon toed

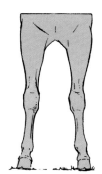

Base wide

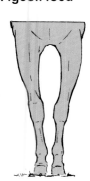

Base narrow

Splay footed or pigeon toed, where the toes turn out or in below the fetlock, are more serious faults. Such animals have an altered action, tending to paddle or 'dish'. These defects put extra strain on the fetlock and pastern joints, which can be a cause of arthritis. They also lead to wear of the foot or shoe, on the opposite side to the way the foot is turned.

Base wide (feet set too far apart), puts more weight on the inside of the foot, which means that the inside of the limb is subjected to strain.

Base narrow (feet too close together), strains the outside of the limb.

Hindlegs

Hindleg defects cause similar problems to those of the forelegs.

Cow hocked: The hocks turn inward, which also makes the toes turn out. This can be one of the most problematic hindlimb conformations because of the strain on the hock joint, which can lead to spavin.

Bow legged (hocks too far outward), also places excessive strain on the limb.

Base wide and base narrow place strain on the inside or the outside of the limb, respectively.

Hindleg defects

Cow hocked

Bow legged

Base wide

Base narrow

Back view
When viewed from behind, an imaginary line dropped from the point of the buttock should pass through the centre of the hock, fetlock joint and foot. Like the forelimbs, the distance between the lines should stay the same all the way down the legs.

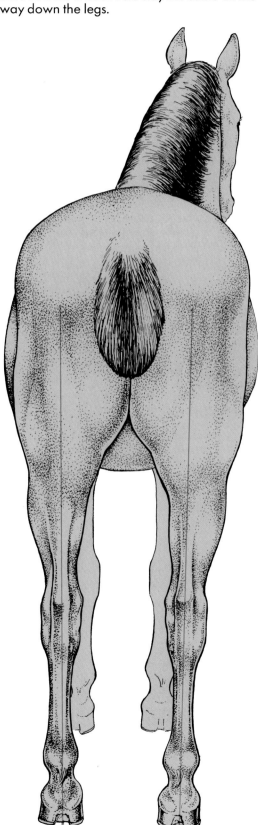

ASSESSING CONFORMATION
To assess a pony's conformation properly you need someone else to hold him. The pony should stand on a hard, level surface with his forelegs and hindlegs together (this is known as 'standing square').

Look at him carefully from directly in front and from directly behind — standing about 4.5m (15ft) away. Check that the two sides of the body are evenly balanced and well proportioned. Look at the width of the chest and hindquarters, and then examine the fore and hindlimbs.

Note whether or not the limbs are straight and how they are placed in relation to imaginary lines from the point of the shoulder and point of the buttock.

Conformation 2: side view

Faults in back conformation affect the horse's appearance and balance – especially when he is ridden. They may also make the back weak. There are a number of serious limb defects, which can cause lameness.

Back conformation

The normal outline of the back dips slightly. A very *hollow* ('sway') *back* is a sign of weakness and is liable to lead to back injuries. It can also be a sign of old age. *Roach back*, in which the back actually curves upward, reduces the athletic ability of the horse. It also causes problems in finding a correctly fitting saddle.

A horse with a *short back* has a tendency to strike his forelegs with his hindlegs while moving (called 'over-reaching'), while a *long back* tends to be weak. Some horses have prominent bones along the back (*razorbacked*). This is more common in old horses.

The withers *should* be prominent, as this shows that there is a firm support for the neck muscles. If they are very narrow, the horse is likely to suffer from pressure sores (saddle galls), and it may be difficult to find a saddle that fits comfortably.

Forelimbs

When viewed from the side, there should be a straight line running from the middle of the shoulder blade, down the forearm, and through the middle of the knees and fetlock. Problems can occur if the line is not straight.

Stands under in front: The leg is angled too far back. This tends to shorten the horse's strides, making him catch his toes and stumble, and causes excessive wear of the leg joints.

Camped in front: The leg is angled too far forward. At each stride the horse is landing on the back of his feet. This places excessive weight on the heels, and can cause laminitis and navicular disease.

Back at the knee: The centre of the knee runs behind the line. This is rarer, but more serious as it can lead to strained ligaments and small ('chip') fractures of the knee bones.

Over at the knee: The centre of the knee runs in front of the line. This puts less strain on the flexor tendons.

Hindlimbs

If you look at the hindlegs from the side, a line dropped from the point of the buttock should pass through the hock, down the back of the leg to the fetlock joint. Very few horses have this ideal conformation.

Camped behind: The hock and fetlock lie behind the line, making the pasterns very straight and prone to wear.

Stands under behind: The fetlock is in front of the line. This is usually associated with sickle hocks.

Sickle hocks: The hocks are excessively angled and weak, leading to strains of the joint. This conformation is also called 'curby hocks', because it tends to cause a hock problem known as curb.

Straight hocks: The hocks are subjected to strain, commonly causing bog spavin (swelling of the hock joint).

▼ **Eclipse**, shown in this detail of a painting by George Stubbs, is one of the most famous racehorses in history.

Born in 1764, Eclipse was never beaten in his entire career. He was the great-great-grandson of Darley Arabian (one of the three founding sires of the English Thoroughbred), and was thought to have superb conformation for a racehorse.

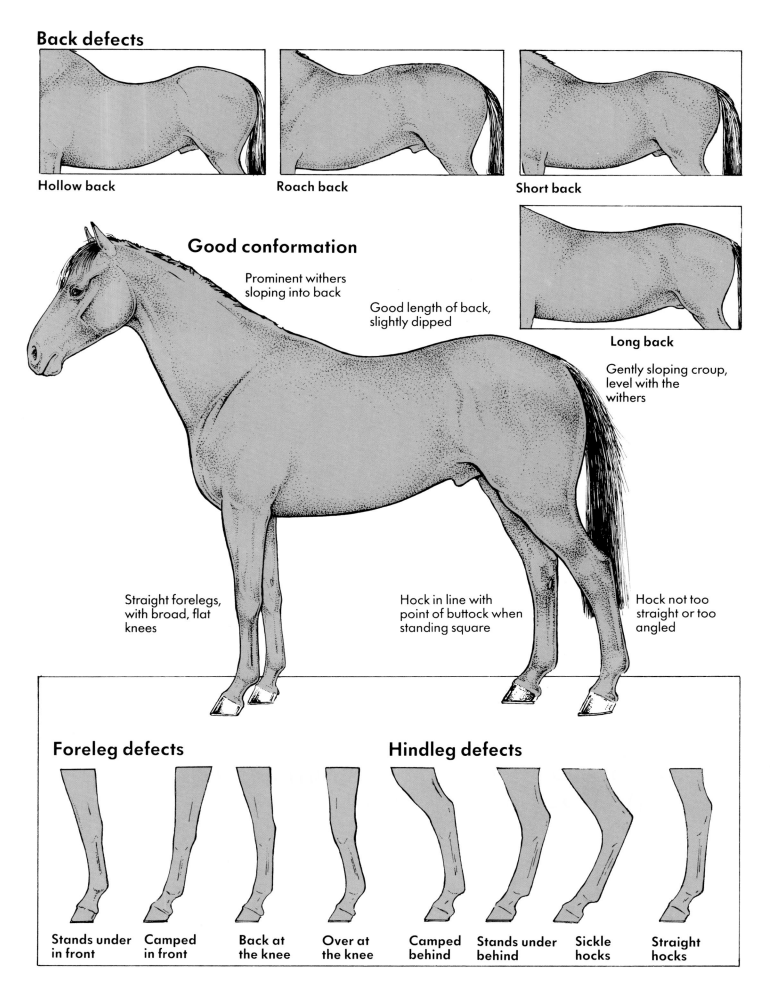

Back defects

Hollow back

Roach back

Short back

Long back

Good conformation

Prominent withers sloping into back

Good length of back, slightly dipped

Gently sloping croup, level with the withers

Straight forelegs, with broad, flat knees

Hock in line with point of buttock when standing square

Hock not too straight or too angled

Foreleg defects

Stands under in front

Camped in front

Back at the knee

Over at the knee

Hindleg defects

Camped behind

Stands under behind

Sickle hocks

Straight hocks

All about hooves

The horse's foot consists of everything within the hoof. Hooves are box-like protective shells and help absorb shock to the legs created when the horse moves.

How is the hoof designed?

The hoof is made up of three parts – the **sole**, **wall** and **frog**.

The sole should be arched and is designed to take weight from above – a well-formed sole shouldn't touch the ground. A **white line** runs around its rim where the sole meets the hoof wall.

The hoof wall is formed at the coronet where horny tissue mixes with special skin-like cells to form the hard hoof wall. This wall is like our nails. But, unlike us, the horse balances and moves around on his tip toes!

The hoof wall has an inner layer of laminae ('fingers' of bone). These inter-lace with a second set of laminae which are attached to the **pedal bone** and lock the hoof firmly into place.

The frog: At the **heel**, the hoof wall turns inward toward the frog, forming the **bars** of the foot. When these make contact with the ground they give slightly, helping to absorb some of the impact.

A well-shaped frog touches the ground as the horse moves and presses upward against the large, fatty pad, known as the **plantar cushion**.

Blood enters and leaves the foot by a **digital artery** and vein on either side of the leg. Two nerves run alongside these vessels, carrying any sensation into the deeper layers of the foot.

How a horse moves

The **pedal joint** lies within the hoof. This acts like a hinge, linking the pedal

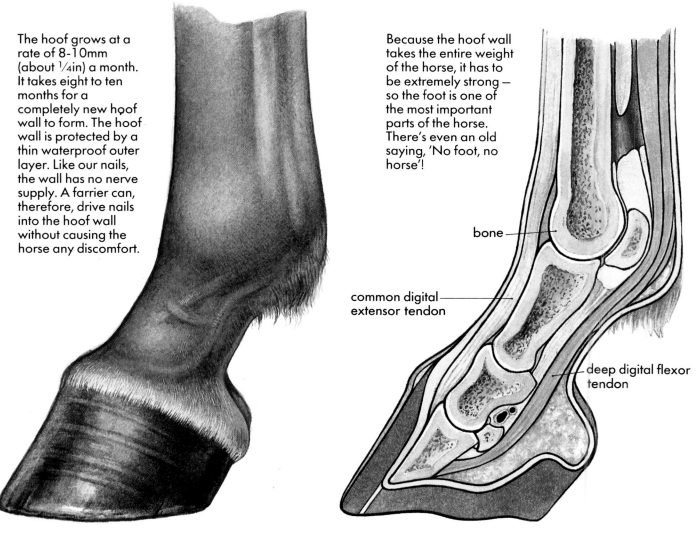

Outside of the foot

The hoof grows at a rate of 8-10mm (about 1/4in) a month. It takes eight to ten months for a completely new hoof wall to form. The hoof wall is protected by a thin waterproof outer layer. Like our nails, the wall has no nerve supply. A farrier can, therefore, drive nails into the hoof wall without causing the horse any discomfort.

Cross-section of the foot

Because the hoof wall takes the entire weight of the horse, it has to be extremely strong – so the foot is one of the most important parts of the horse. There's even an old saying, 'No foot, no horse'!

bone

common digital extensor tendon

deep digital flexor tendon

bone to the **short pastern bone**, and makes it possible for the horse to move his foot.

Two large tendons (sinews) move the pedal bone. One (the **common digital extensor**) enters the hoof at the front, while the other (the **deep digital flexor**) runs down the back of the pastern to enter the hoof at the heels.

Behind the pedal bone is a second small bone, known as the **navicular bone**, over which the deep digital flexor tendon runs. When the tendon stretches over this bone it helps to absorb further the shock of impact.

The horse's weight is taken by the hoof wall, not the sole. For brief moments during a jump or gallop, the whole weight of the horse (around 500kg/1100lb) is supported on a single foreleg showing the tremendous strength of the horse's hooves.

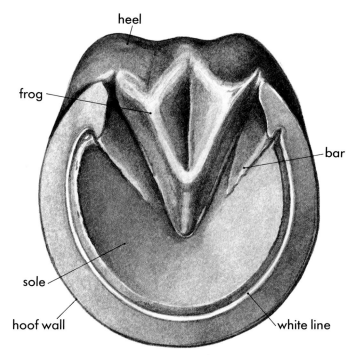

Ground surface of the hoof

Circulation in the foot

Blood is circulated around the foot by the digital artery and vein, which run alongside each other. When the frog makes contact with the ground it presses upward against the plantar cushion which in turn pumps blood back up the horse's legs.

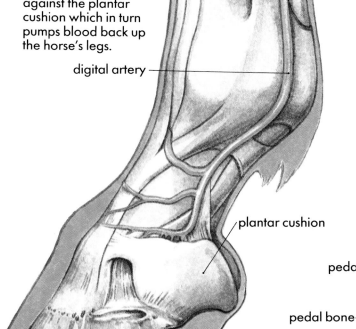

The bones of the foot

The horse's foot can be compared to our fingers. The hoof wall is like our finger nails, the tips of our fingers are the equivalent of the pedal bone, our middle bone is like the short pastern and our third bone is similar to the long pastern.

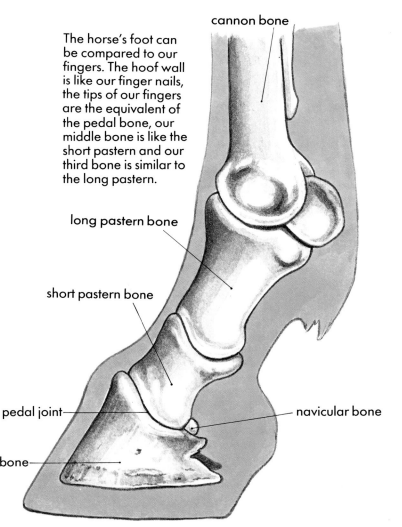

15

The anatomy

The body of the horse is not really designed to suit the needs of a rider. In the wild, horses gallop in short bursts and only jump to escape danger. So the two most popular tasks we ask our horses to perform are also the most demanding.

Simply sitting on a horse puts strain on him and affects his balance. The horse has to adjust to your weight whenever you ride. But by riding correctly – and sensitively – you can make life much easier for him.

The framework
The anatomy (skeleton) is the framework of bones which protects the internal organs like the heart and lungs. It also supports the muscles and helps to provide movement. It is made up of about 210 bones (excluding the tail).

The spine
The horse has a rigid spine and a heavy body, unlike other agile animals. Because of this the joints are under strain when he moves, particularly when he gallops over several miles or jumps.

To cope with this, the ends of each bone are made up of hard, dense cells. These are covered by cartilage (padding) which acts as a shock absorber and protects the horse as his hooves hit the ground.

The horse has a weak point at the end of the rib cage and before the pelvis begins – a small row of vertebrae are the only supporting bones. Never sit here or put weight on this point.

The limbs
Joints in the hindlegs are angled. They help to propel the horse forward so all movement begins from here. After a jump the horse comes down on the forelegs which, with the shoulders, absorb most of the shock.

The head and neck
The skull is long to accommodate the teeth. The neck is also long, and together they enable the horse to reach short grass or leafy branches!

A horse's weight shifts forward when he lowers his head, and shifts backward when he lifts it. You can feel this when you're riding. You are automatically tipped forward when the horse puts his head down and, if he tosses his head up, your weight goes backward.

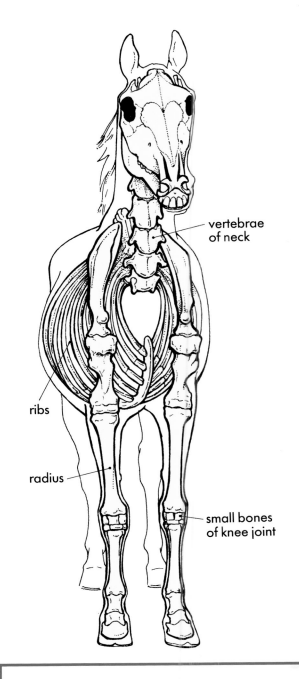

vertebrae of neck

ribs

radius

small bones of knee joint

The spine and speed
Although we think of horses as being speedy animals, they're actually quite slow relative to their size. The horse has a rigid spine which gives it a limited degree of movement. Racehorses can reach about 64kmph (40mph) over a short period, but compare this with the cheetah — an animal less than half its size.

The cheetah can run at 113kmph (70mph), making it the fastest animal on earth. This is largely due to its flexible spine which curves up and down when it runs. The leg bones swivel with the spine. So the cheetah can increase its speed and lengthen its stride, alternately extending all four legs and bunching them underneath its body. A single bound can extend a massive 7m (23ft).

What the skeleton looks like

A side view of the horse's anatomy shows clearly the strong, interlocking bones in the legs which provide the power to move fast. The bones in the forelegs (best seen from the front) take the strain after a jump.

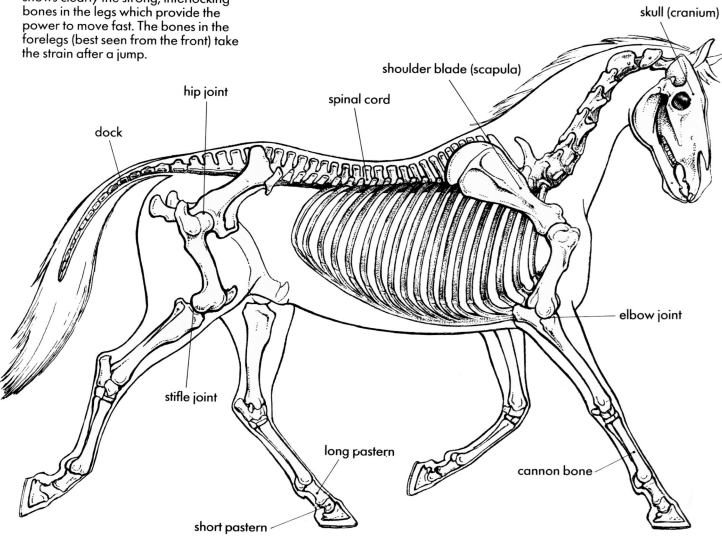

skull (cranium)

shoulder blade (scapula)

spinal cord

hip joint

dock

elbow joint

stifle joint

long pastern

cannon bone

short pastern

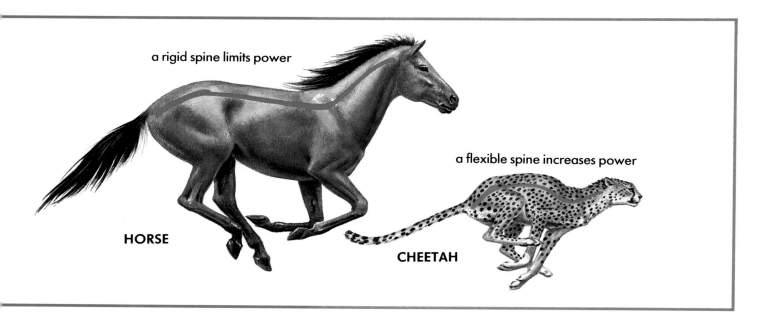

a rigid spine limits power

a flexible spine increases power

HORSE

CHEETAH

Muscles and movement

SPEED OR ENDURANCE?

Some horses perform best at speed events, others excel at endurance competitions – just like athletes who are good at either sprinting or long-distance running.

The make-up of the fibre in the muscle determines where a horse's strength lies. There are two main groups – 'slow twitch' and 'fast twitch' fibres.

Slow twitch fibres contract slowly and require plenty of oxygen. They are important in long-distance performance.

Fast twitch fibres contract quickly and do not need as much oxygen. They are important for speed events.

Muscle fibre is determined at birth and cannot be altered by training.

SMOOTH MUSCLE

A different type of muscle, smooth muscle, is found in the arteries and bowel wall. Smooth muscle enables the arteries to pump blood around the body and helps the bowel wall push food along by contracting.

Smooth muscle is also in the airways to the lungs allowing a horse to cough if he is allergic, for instance, to the dust in his bedding.

The main purpose of the muscles is to support the horse's weight – about 500kg (1100lb). The muscles also give a horse the power to move around quickly and over long distances.

What are muscles?

Muscles are made up of thousands of minute fibres which create energy by contracting.

When standing, only a few of the fibres in the muscles are needed to hold up the weight. But when a horse is involved in strenuous exercise or work, all the fibres in the muscle contract to meet the animal's needs.

The main muscles are situated on the shoulders, trunk, loins and hindquarters. The moving parts, such as the legs, have very little heavy muscle tissue. This cuts down their weight and reduces

the level of wind resistance.

The horse's speed and stamina – which come from the muscles – have played a major part in the horse's survival over millions of years. The strong and finely co-ordinated system of muscles has given it the power to escape danger fast.

How the muscles work

Most of the horse's muscles are attached to its bones by fibres known as ligaments. But in the case of the legs the energy is transferred from the muscles in the forearm and thigh to the limbs by long fibrous bands called tendons.

Tendons run over pulley-like structures such as the sesamoid bone in the fetlock and the navicular bone in the hoof. These act as supports and increase the power that the muscles can exert.

The main areas of muscle

This diagram shows the outer muscles of a horse. Beneath these muscles lies a deeper, hidden layer which also helps provide movement and energy.

The main force which propels the horse forward comes from the **hindquarters**. This thick mass of complex muscle covering the buttocks does most work during galloping.

The horse's **skin** has many more muscles than ours. This gives horses and ponies the enviable ability to twitch any part of their body to dislodge flies!

The main energy comes from the pendulum-like motion of the **legs**.

Strong **back muscles** hold the back bones together tightly.

Horse power?

The idea of 'horsepower' in cars dates from the earliest days of motorized transport. Horsepower was calculated on an average horse lifting about 15 tons over 30cm (1ft) in one minute. This 12 horsepower racing car — pictured in 1906 — was unbeaten at 40 miles an hour!

The importance of exercise

When the muscle contracts to provide energy, waste products are produced.

One of these waste products, lactic acid, can cause fatigue if it is allowed to accumulate.

To prevent this from happening the muscles must have an efficient blood supply. This helps the process of absorbing oxygen and getting rid of waste products.

Regular exercise improves the blood supply to the muscles by keeping the blood moving around the body. This maintains a healthy circulation and keeps the muscles in good shape.

Powerful **neck muscles** are necessary to lift the relatively heavy head from the ground after feeding.

Strong **jaw muscles** enable the horse to crop its food and grind it thoroughly.
Smaller muscles on the face also help to move the ears and eyes to detect danger.

The **chest** is attached to the shoulder blades by muscles which help to absorb shock during movement.

Efficient **rib muscles** are important for breathing, but the diaphragm, a strong muscular structure contained within the chest, is also essential because it helps expand the chest.

The **forelegs** take most of the weight, and play an important role in absorbing shock.

★ **NON-STOP HEARTBEAT**
The heart is composed of extremely strong muscle — cardiac muscle — so that it can perform the arduous task of pumping blood around the body.

To keep the blood moving, the muscle in the heart has to expand and contract non-stop. Even when a horse is at rest, the heart beats between 30—40 times a minute.

Horses have no control over the muscle in the heart. But it automatically contracts more often if a horse is involved in exercise or if he needs to escape danger. At a gallop the heart beats about 220 times a minute.

How the blood circulates

The blood has the important task of carrying oxygen and nourishment to all the cells within the horse's body. It also plays a vital role in preventing disease and helping to keep a horse healthy.

The contents of the blood

Blood is made up of liquids and solids. The liquid, called serum, carries the solids around the body and takes waste products to the **kidneys** to be discharged.

The solids are divided into two parts – red blood cells and white blood cells. The red blood cells transport oxygen round the body and carry waste gases from the tissues to the lungs. White blood cells, on the other hand, act as an army helping to combat the enemy – disease.

How blood pumps round

The horse has a highly efficient **heart** which acts as a pump. It sends blood to every part of the body.

Blood leaves the heart and flows toward the **lungs** where it absorbs oxygen. It then returns to the heart and begins its journey through a major network of **arteries**.

The thick muscular walls of the **aorta**, the main artery leading from the heart, squeeze blood along into smaller arteries. These eventually link up with minute vessels called **capillaries**. Here oxygen and nutrients are absorbed and waste products discharged.

The **liver** acts as a filter sorting out and storing nutrients. Worn-out red blood cells pass into the **spleen** where they are destroyed.

Capillaries connect the arteries to veins. Once the oxygen has been absorbed the blood starts its homeward journey to the heart through the **veins**.

Veins have thin walls with little muscle in them and so rely on movement of the surrounding tissues to squeeze blood back along them. They

The vital organs requiring oxygen

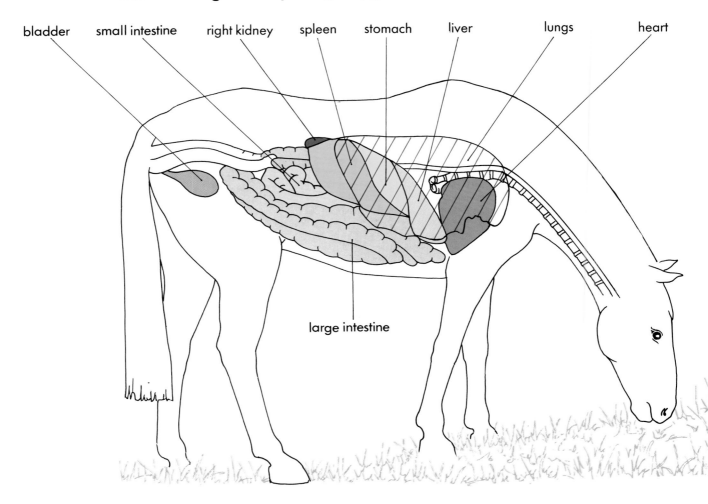

bladder small intestine right kidney spleen stomach liver lungs heart

large intestine

also have valves which allow blood to flow in one direction only. So when a horse puts his head down to graze, the blood does not rush to his head. It continues on its way back to the heart.

Additional help

Blood returning to the heart from the feet has an uphill struggle. It tends to collect in the feet.

To overcome this, there is an in-built pump within the foot which helps force blood back up the legs. When a horse's hoof hits the ground, the V-shaped frog makes contact and presses against the shock-absorbing plantar cushion lying beneath it. This squeezes the veins in the foot and helps pump blood up the leg.

Painful parts

When a part of the body is deprived of its normal blood supply the cells die and it becomes extremely painful. Colic is frequently caused by the lack of blood supply to a part of the **bowel**. This in turn is often caused by a blockage in a blood vessel.

Another most painful condition in horses and ponies – laminitis – results from changes in the blood supply to the feet.

Regular exercise is one of the keys to maintaining an efficient circulation system – this is what is meant by getting a horse fit. It helps improve the movement of blood in the feet and keeps the muscles well supplied with oxygen.

★ **HEAVY HEART**
A horse's heart weighs about 4k (8½lb) and is relatively large compared to the size of its body. Compared to this, the human heart is light – between 300-350gm (10-12oz).

Its size and efficiency usually determine a horse's powers of speed and stamina – a small horse with a large heart can often out-run a larger one with a smaller heart.

The heart, therefore, can have an effect on the performance of a race horse.

For instance, the heart of the legendary unbeaten race horse, 'Eclipse' weighed over 6.5k (14lb)!

Veins and arteries

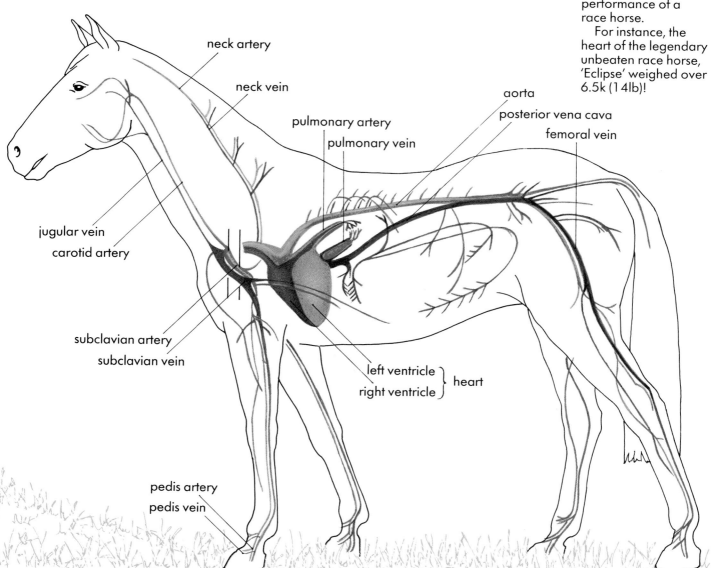

neck artery

neck vein

pulmonary artery

pulmonary vein

aorta

posterior vena cava

femoral vein

jugular vein

carotid artery

subclavian artery

subclavian vein

left ventricle ⎫
right ventricle ⎭ heart

pedis artery

pedis vein

How the horse digests food

Horses and ponies have an efficient digestive system designed to cope with their natural diet – grass.

How the horse eats

Grass is fairly indigestible so, for a horse to get enough goodness out of it, he needs to eat large amounts. But the stomach is so small that he has to eat little and often.

The horse's stomach works best when it is two-thirds full. An over-full stomach can cause pain (colic) and slows down the process of passing food from the stomach into the small intestine.

In a field, horses feed throughout the day. Stable-kept horses should be given frequent small feeds to imitate their natural pattern – never give a horse a large feed that he cannot cope with.

A horse has sharp front (incisor) teeth which enable him to graze tight to the ground. Horses also have mobile lips, which they use as 'fingers' to pick up small grains. The tongue moves food to the teeth at the back of the mouth where it is crushed thoroughly before being swallowed and passed down the **digestive tract**.

Breaking down the food

The grass is washed down with plenty of liquid to help reduce the food to a pulp. Horses produce vast quantities of saliva a day – about 10-12 litres (2-2½ gallons). Compare this with the amount of

! RECOGNIZING
● COLIC
Horses have an exceptionally sensitive nerve supply. Even the slightest twinge of indigestion causes severe pain (colic).

This makes it very difficult to tell whether or not something serious is wrong. All colic should be treated as an emergency. If a pony looks as though he's in pain, call your vet right away.

COLOUR CODING
The parts of the horse's digestive system are colour coded so that you can easily distinguish them.

- ▢ digestive tract
- ▢ stomach
- ▢ small intestine
- ▢ caecum (pronounced *sea-cum*)
- ▢ large colon
- ▢ small colon
- ▢ rectum

Four to one

The horse has an extremely small stomach for its size. It holds betwen 8 and 15 litres (1½-3½ gallons). This is very different from the other main group of grass-eaters — ruminants — who chew their food twice. The cow, for example, has four stomachs which hold from 140 to 235 litres (30-50 gallons).

The cow's stomach occupies the left flank; the other organs the right. So that all the organs are visible, the stomach has been drawn further forward and to the right of its true position.

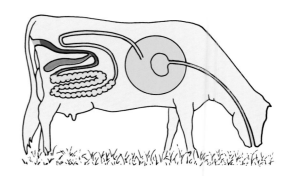

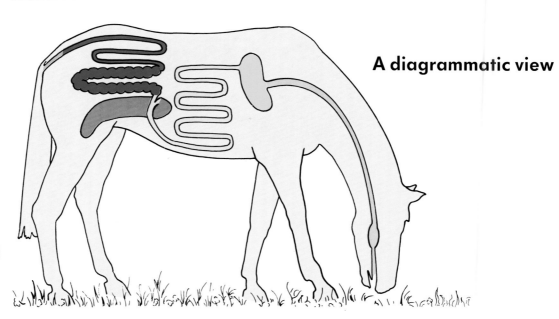

A diagrammatic view

The digestive system

The digestive system of the horse and cow shown in diagram form on this page illustrate just how much smaller the horse's stomach is compared to that of the cow.

The cow's four stomachs hold about 20 times as much food as that of the horse. This is because food breaks down in the cow's rumen, the biggest of its four stomachs. In the horse, this process takes place in the large intestine, which is correspondingly bigger than that of the cow.

saliva we produce – between 1-1½ litres (2-3 pints) a day.

When food reaches the **stomach** and **small intestine**, digestive juices are added. Some nutrients are absorbed in the small intestine – particularly sugars and proteins – from concentrated food such as nuts and oats.

Food then moves on and breaks down further in the large intestine (which consists of the **caecum**, the **large colon** and the **small colon** and passes into the **rectum**.

The horse's caecum (pronounced sea-cum) is the equivalent of the human appendix. But our appendix has become unnecessary over the years as grass is no longer a part of our diet.

The large intestine can hold 80 to 120 litres (18-26 gallons) of fermenting food. Here, bacteria break up the grass into nutrients that the horse can absorb. The bacteria even produce some vitamins themselves, so the horse has its own built-in vitamin factory! Bacteria are absorbed with the dissolved nutrients, at the end of the large intestine.

The end result

Once the fluid has been absorbed, the horse passes waste matter through the rectum. Droppings should be soft enough to break up on hitting the ground.

If stabled horses eat too much dry food, don't have enough to drink or lack exercise their bowel movements may slow down. This allows more time for fluid to be absorbed, makes the dropping hard, and can cause constipation. So it is important to give laxative foods (such as a bran mash) to stabled horses before a day off, or if they cannot be exercised due to illness.

DID YOU KNOW?
A horse is unable to vomit because of the anatomy of the back of the mouth. If a horse chokes, or its stomach becomes swollen (this happens in some cases of colic) food must be brought back through the nostrils.

All the words in **heavy print** are shown on the diagrams.

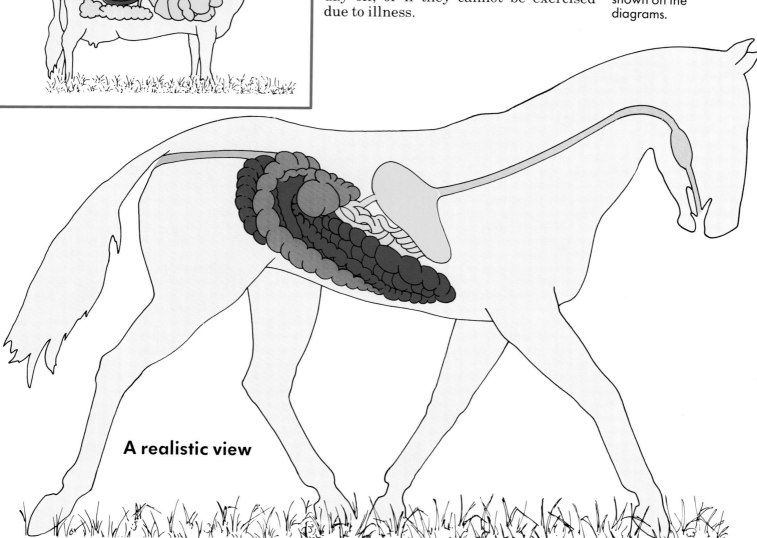

A realistic view

Sight and hearing

In the wild, a horse is naturally defensive. When threatened, his instinct is to escape. But he needs advance warning to run away in enough time to avoid the danger.

The horse's eyes and ears work together to give this warning. The eyes are geared for sideways vision, backed up by acute hearing.

Seeing sideways

Horses have prominent eyes which are set well apart on the sides of the face. This means that a horse can see almost all around his body with one or other eye and can detect danger.

However, this eye position presents a problem. Most of a horse's vision is one eyed and he cannot see directly in front or behind – he has a blind spot.

The sensitive ear

To help their sight, horses have extremely sensitive hearing. They can locate the *exact* source of sound, picking up softer noises than the human ear.

A horse has 16 muscles controlling each ear and can move his ears separately toward the sound, rather than moving the whole head. The funnel shape of the ears helps to make sounds seem louder and clearer.

▼ **The position of a horse's eyes** limits sight directly in front and behind.

When a horse looks straight ahead with his head in its normal resting position, the eyes focus on a point about 2m (7ft) from his muzzle. A horse cannot see immediately in front of him. This area is known as the blind spot.

► **Horses sometimes wear blinkers** to restrict their sideways vision.

Blinkers stop a horse being distracted from the work in hand and help to keep his concentration.

▼ **Horses cannot focus** on obstacles straight in front of them. If a horse cannot see or remember a fence, he may refuse to jump (below). Once he has investigated the obstacle (below right), he should jump clear.

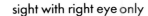
sight with right eye only

unsighted

◄ **When startled** by a strange or unusual noise a horse often prepares for flight. He pricks up his ears, points them toward the sound (left), tries to identify it and then decides whether or not he needs to take flight (below).

unsighted

sight with left eye only

► **Horses can move their ears** to point in every direction around their body.

This mare points her ears backward to check what is behind her, so that she is always ready to protect her foal. The foal in turn listens to his mother to check that everything is safe.

Touch and sensation

Sensory nerves, which respond to touch, heat, cold and pain, are scattered throughout the horse's skin. But a horse's sensitivity varies over the different parts of its body, depending on the number of nerves supplied to each area.

STANDING STILL

A horse's sensitive skin can be helpful in restraining a naughty horse.

You can make a horse stand still for a few moments by pinching a small fold of skin in the middle of the neck.

How horses feel

The nose and muzzle are so sensitive that horses can use them much as we use our fingers. Nerves in the highly sensitive whiskers around the muzzle send messages to the brain whenever they come into contact with something. These messages help the horse to judge how far away an object is and whether or not it may be dangerous. Similar hairs surround and protect the eyes.

Horses also have extremely sensitive backs. They can easily detect flies landing on them and, if you run your finger or a brush gently along a horse's spine, it often dips down in reaction to the contact. Indeed, some horses have such sensitive skin that they dip their backs whenever the saddle is put on. This is known as a 'cold back'.

Continual pressure on a sensitive

▼ **Scratching** an itchy area can be difficult for ponies. This Dartmoor pony finds the solution by rubbing himself against a rock.

area tends to dull feeling. For this reason, pulling at the bit deadens the bars of the mouth and can make a horse insensitive and unresponsive.

Feeling the heat

Nerves in the skin are not only sensitive to touch. They also respond to heat and cold. When the skin is hot, its blood vessels open up to lose heat. More fluid enters the sweat glands to produce extra sweat and so help cool the horse.

In summer, horses also change their coat and the hair lies flat to prevent a warming layer of air from being trapped between the hairs.

Out in the cold

In cold weather, the horse's nerve centre responds to produce the opposite effect. The vessels close up and produce less sweat. If the temperature drops even lower, the hairs stand on end, trapping air in the coat and providing a warm, insulating blanket.

In really cold weather, ponies often indulge in a bit of do-it-yourself 'loft insulation'. They roll about in mud so that they become caked in a messy but effective coat that helps prevent heat loss from the surface of the skin!

◄ **The long sensitive whiskers** help horses determine the texture of the pasture when grazing. This Haflinger has been furrowing in the snow for fresh green grass.

▲ **In the heat** of the midday sun, a herd of Mustangs seek shelter in the shade of trees. Horses can suffer from sunburn if they have any fleshmarks (unpigmented skin) on their coat.

DID YOU KNOW?
When horses moult in summer, their coats produce a waterproofing oil known as sebum. This protects the coat and helps keep out the rain so the horse stays cool but dry.

◄ **During the winter**, horses usually grow a thick coat to protect them from the low temperatures. In extreme cold, the long hair on these ponies stands on end to trap air and so warm up their bodies.

Smell and taste

The senses of smell and taste play a very important part in the lives of horses because they act as a warning system. Smell is useful for sorting out the familiar from the unknown and taste helps a horse to distinguish between healthy and harmful food or water.

Recognizing each other

A horse uses its acute sense of smell to investigate strange objects. When a pony enters an unfamiliar stable or paddock the first thing he does is sniff and snort at his new surroundings.

Horses recognize their friends and rivals through body smell – each individual has its own scent. Horses usually sniff each other's breath when they greet one another. This is the equine equivalent of a hand-shake.

Scent is particularly important in the bond between mare and foal. A mare works out which foal belongs to her by the smell it gives off.

Horses even get used to a person's natural odour and any unusual smell such as perfume confuses them and can upset them.

When a horse wants to study a smell more closely, he takes a deep breath, raises his head and curls the top lip upward, over the nostrils, to trap the smell in his nose. This behaviour is known as 'flehmen'.

In the wild

Horses can detect smells over long distances. A stallion can pick up the scent of a mare that is in season when she is up to 600m (780yds) away. Horses can tell where there is water from a long way away as well.

Smells also form a part of boundary marking. Horses deposit droppings and urine around their personal territory so that others can recognize the borders and avoid 'trespassing'.

A horse's strong sense of smell discourages it from grazing near droppings because they send out an unpleasant odour. This is important in preventing the spread of worms.

The sweet tooth

Horses choose their food firstly by smell and then by taste. Their muzzles act like

▲ **Treat your horse** to sweet titbits every now and then. But try not to give him too many because he'll expect them all the time and it may make him bad mannered.

► **Smell** is one of the horse's most important senses. A horse recognizes his friends by their body smell. Here a couple of wild horses sniff each other's breath in recognition.

fingers in helping to sort out what they want to eat and what they want to leave behind.

Having passed the 'sniff' test, food can then be distinguished by its sweet, bitter, sour or salty taste. Generally horses dislike bitter tastes and have a sweet tooth.

Because of this, they usually love sugar lumps and are also often very fond of sugar-beet. They also like unusual or spicy tastes, including peppermints and ginger.

The 'taste' test is a final safety mechanism: poisonous plants, such as ragwort, yew and laburnum, taste extremely bitter and are quickly rejected. Even if a horse or pony is tempted to take a bite of something dangerous, in most cases he spits it out straight away.

▲ **Although horses do not eat buttercups** from choice, they sometimes munch them with a mouthful of grass because these flowers do not taste as bitter as other poisonous plants. Fortunately buttercups are only harmful if they are eaten in great quantities so the odd one will not upset a pony.

▼ **Horses enjoy all types of titbits** from carrots and apples to hard mints and treats. Horses have an exceptionally sweet tooth – but never give a horse soft mints as he cannot cope with chewy foods.

peppermint treats

carrots

carrot treats

apples

hard mints

All about teeth

The horse's teeth are well designed to cope with his main source of food – grass. Although constant chewing and grinding of grass wears away the tooth surface, horses' teeth continue to grow throughout their lives – unlike ours, which do not grow at all once they have fully developed. Growth normally occurs in a tooth at the same rate at which it is being worn away. This means that the teeth always *appear* to be the same, unchanging length.

How the teeth work

The horse's teeth begin the digestive process by cutting and crushing the food, so it is in a suitable state for the rest of the digestive system to work on. A horse's front teeth (incisors) act like very sharp scissors, cutting the grass and enabling the animal to graze very close to the ground.

After it has been cut, the grass is transferred to the back of the mouth by the tongue, which is very mobile. Here the grass is thoroughly ground between the cheek teeth before being swallowed.

The horse's teeth

All adult horses have at least 36 teeth – 12 front teeth (incisors) and 24 cheek teeth (molars). Male horses usually have four extra teeth, called 'tushes' (canines).
The front teeth (incisors): There are six incisor teeth in each jaw (upper and lower). They must meet exactly for the animal to eat effectively. When the upper teeth are in front of the lower ones ('parrot' mouth), or the other way round ('under-shot'), it is difficult for the animal to graze properly.
Cheek teeth (premolars and molars): There are six cheek teeth on each side of the upper jaw, and the same number in the lower jaw. Technically, there are three

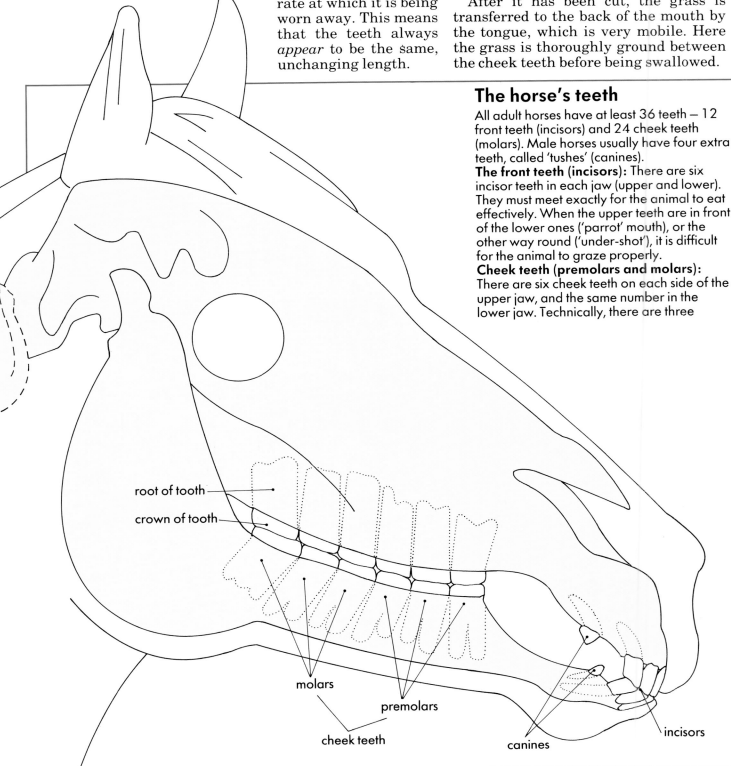

root of tooth

crown of tooth

molars

premolars

cheek teeth

canines

incisors

► **Not just for eating:** These two horses are using their teeth for mutual grooming. This is where they scratch each other's withers, back or the top of the tail. Not only does this relieve itching in difficult-to-reach places, but it is a sign of friendship and trust.

premolar teeth and three *molar* teeth, but there is no real difference between them.

These teeth are covered with a hard substance called enamel, but the grinding surface is folded into many ridges and crevices in which there is an even harder material known as cement.

Canine teeth (tushes): Stallions and geldings usually develop small canine teeth at four years old, but three out of four mares do not possess them at all. They are found in the space between the front teeth and the cheek teeth. As they do not meet with the same tooth in the opposite jaw, they cannot be used for eating, and may become quite sharp.

Teeth and diet

The horse is a *herbivore* (he eats grass and other vegetation) and the tiger is a *carnivore* (meat-eater). Because of their opposite diets, their teeth are shaped completely differently. The horse's incisors (front teeth) are well-developed chisels for cutting grass — unlike those of the tiger, which are tiny and of little importance. In contrast, the tiger has large, pointed canines for catching and holding prey. The horse's canines are either small or absent because they have no eating function.

Prehistoric teeth

The earliest prehistoric horses lived in swamps some 60-70 million years ago. Here they ate juicy fruits and succulent plants. These animals had very small, soft teeth which were well suited to their diet. Over millions of years, the climate changed. The swamps were replaced by dry plains where there was only a sparse covering of much tougher food material – grass.

During this period the teeth of the horse's ancestors gradually altered to cope with their new diet. The small soft teeth were replaced by much bigger ones with a tougher grinding surface. The horse's facial bones lengthened to make room for these large teeth. Powerful jaw muscles also developed, so the horse could crush the grass to pulp.

Wolf teeth

A few horses have extra, tiny cheek teeth, known as 'wolf' teeth. They lie in front of the upper cheek teeth and, rarely, in front of the lower cheek teeth as well.

These teeth can be very sharp. When the bit pulls the horse's cheeks against them, the cheeks may be cut and become sore. This can make the horse unwilling to respond to his rider's instructions. So these 'useless' teeth are sometimes removed by the vet, under a painless local anaesthetic.

RASPING THE TEETH
If the surface of the tooth wears down unevenly, the edges may become sharp and cut the cheeks and tongue, so the horse cannot chew his food properly.

When this happens, a vet must 'rasp' the teeth (file them down to make the surfaces level). Tooth problems are very common in old horses, and their teeth should be checked regularly.

Telling a horse's age

Horses' front teeth (incisors) show characteristic signs of wear with age. These changes can be used to tell a pony's age fairly accurately up to the age of 8. Beyond this, it is only possible to give an estimate, so horses and ponies over 8 are often described as 'aged'.

Milk teeth

A pony has a full set of six temporary *(milk)* incisor teeth in each jaw by the time he is 9 months old. The two innermost teeth in each jaw are called *centrals*, those on each side of them are called *laterals* (or *middle* incisors), and those at the corners of the mouth are known as *corners*.

Between 2½ and 4½ years, the temporary teeth are replaced by permanent ones. You should be able to distinguish the white, shell-like milk teeth from the bigger, yellowish, adult ones, when ageing young horses.

The tables

The next step is to inspect the grinding surfaces of the teeth (called *tables*). The outline of the tables changes with age – it is oval in young horses (5 years), becomes circular by 8, then more and more triangular.

In the middle of the tables of young horses is a hole known as the *infundibulum*. As the teeth wear down, this hole becomes less obvious and eventually disappears. Wear also exposes a

---

Birth to 4 weeks

The two innermost temporary incisors ('centrals') are either present at birth, or emerge soon afterwards. These teeth have a large hole in the centre – the *infundibulum*.

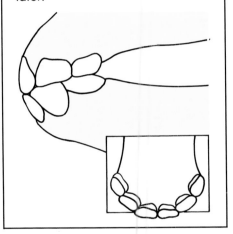

4 to 6 weeks

The second pair of temporary incisors ('laterals' or middle incisors) have now emerged through the gums on each side of the centrals.

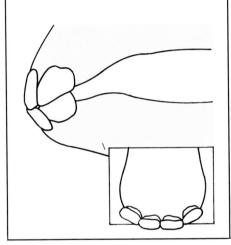

6 to 9 months

The third pair of temporary incisors ('corners') come through at about 9 months, but are not 'fully in wear' (meet with the opposite teeth) until 3 to 5 months later.

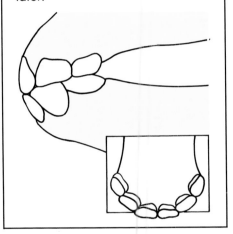

---

6 years

The infundibulum has become faint and has almost disappeared from the central teeth. Up to this age, the central incisors meet vertically.

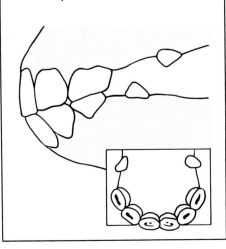

7 years

The upper corner incisors have developed the typical '7 year hook'. The centrals are becoming rounder in outline than the oval shape of younger horses.

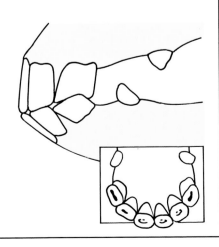

8 years

The black *dental star* is becoming apparent, just in front of the remains of the infundibulum in the centrals and laterals. The teeth now meet at an angle, not vertically.

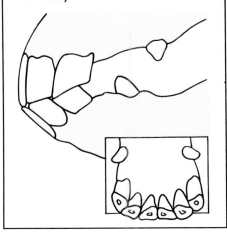

ridge of dentine which is first seen as a black, elongated line in front of the infundibulum at 8 years. This is known as the *dental star*. It becomes progressively more circular as the horse gets older.

Long in the tooth

In young horses (up to 8 years) the teeth meet vertically when viewed from the side. Beyond the age of 8, the angle between upper and lower teeth becomes increasingly more acute, until, at 20, the teeth meet at right angles. In old horses, too, the gums recede from the teeth — they become 'long in the tooth'.

In some horses and ponies (but not all) there is a stained groove on the outer surface of the upper corner incisors. This is known as *Galvayne's groove*. It first appears at the gum at 10, has grown half way down the tooth by 15, and reaches the grinding surface at 20.

Looking at teeth: a tricky business!

3 years
The temporary central incisors are replaced by larger, permanent ones at 2½ years old, but these do not come fully into wear until the horse is 3.

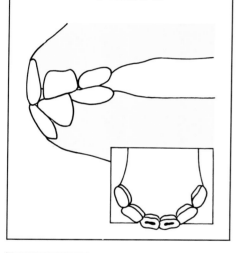

4 years
The temporary lateral (middle) incisors have been lost and replaced by permanent ones at 3½. They will not come fully into wear until the horse is 4 years old.

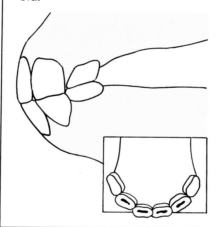

4½ years
The temporary corner incisors are being replaced by permanent ones. The pony will have a complete set of adult teeth when he is 5. The canine teeth ('tushes') have emerged after 4.

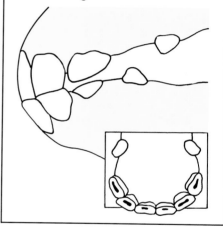

10 years
Dental stars are present in all teeth. The centrals are becoming more triangular in outline. *Galvayne's groove* is just appearing at the gum on the upper corner teeth.

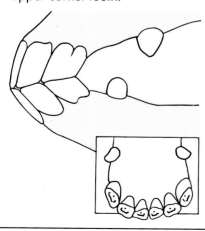

13 years
The infundibulum has just about disappeared from all six teeth. The dental stars are becoming wider and rounder. The teeth are more triangular in outline, and meet at a much greater angle.

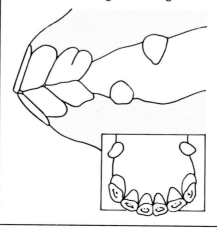

20 years
The angle between the two sets of teeth is now almost 90°. The tables are triangular in outline, and Galvayne's groove has reached the tip of the upper corner teeth.

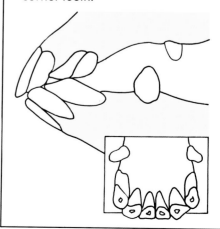

Breeding: the stallion

► **A stallion** uses his sense of smell to test whether or not a mare is ready for mating. When she is, she gives off special scents called pheromones. To study these smells closely, the stallion traps them in his nose by curling his top lip over his nostrils — this is known as 'flehmen'.

▼ **In any herd of horses** only the dominant stallion can mate with the mares. Here he herds his team of mares away from rival males.

Watching a herd of wild horses during the breeding season can be fascinating — particularly if you know how stallions and mares show their attraction for each other.

In a wild herd there is one dominant stallion who has the right to mate with any mature mare. Females can start to breed from about the age of two and they may continue well into their 20's.

The mating season

Horses naturally breed in spring. From late winter the increasing hours of daylight stimulate chemicals called hormones in the bodies of both mares and stallions. These hormones prepare the horses mentally and physically for breeding.

When mares are ready for mating, they give off special scents – called pheromones – from their flanks and

◀▲ **As a stallion woos a mare** he sniffs and nibbles her. If she isn't ready for mating, she might well kick so he takes care never to approach her from behind. If she is ready to mate, she pricks her ears and allows him to nuzzle her.

around their tails. The stallion can detect them from up to a mile away, and when he does pick up a mare's scent the courtship begins. A domesticated stallion acts in exactly the same way and the presence of a mare in season can make him difficult to control for a novice rider.

Courtship

The stallion raises his head, opens his nostrils wide, pricks his ears and sniffs the air. He then walks toward the mare with his neck arched, head tossing and tail raised. He may circle her and follow her around squealing and nickering. Then he sniffs and nibbles her sides, flanks and around her tail. He curls his top lip over his nostrils to trap her smell in his nose.

An experienced stallion always approaches a mare from the side to avoid being kicked if she is not ready to mate. If she is ready, mating often takes place several times until the mare becomes pregnant or 'goes out of season'. When she is pregnant, a mare carries her foal for 11 months.

Rival males

In the wild each male must know his place. The dominant stallion chases out of the herd any outsider trying to take over and any junior male able to mate. He herds his team of mares away from the other males, who often try to approach a mare when the dominant

stallion isn't looking. They even try to steal young mares to start herds of their own. If they are unsuccessful, young males often go around together in 'gangs'. Females, on the other hand, always like to stay in family groups.

Only the strongest, bravest and cleverest stallions win the right to mate – old, defeated stallions often lead solitary lives.

Foaling time

To give foals the best start in life, nature works out the timing of their birth carefully. With the mating season in spring and an 11-month pregnancy, foals are usually born the following spring. The weather is warmer and the grass is growing.

If a foal is born too early, he can suffer badly from harsh weather. There may also be little grass around, which means his mother won't be able to provide enough milk for him.

If a foal is born too late, he may not survive the winter.

Pregnancy in horses can last from 321 days to 361 — nearly a year!

Pregnancy: a new life

A foal starts its long journey into the world when an egg from the mare's ovary meets the sperm from the stallion after mating. From the moment of conception it then takes about 336 days – roughly 11 months – for the foal to develop and grow inside the mare.

This interval of time – known as the gestation period – may not be the same for every mare. Some breeds have a longer gestation period than others: it can be as short as 321 days or as long as 361 days. Sometimes mares of the same breed have different gestation periods – one individual may produce her foals early and another always foal late.

The first signs

About two and a half weeks after conception the mare usually stops showing the signs of coming into season (when she is ready to mate).

In some cases, when the season has finished and the mare has successfully conceived, there may be no obvious changes in her condition until the time of foaling.

Usually, however, it should be obvious that a mare is pregnant. Caring owners know when their mare is not coming into season and whether it is possible that she has conceived.

Mares can be tested for pregnancy by a vet. There are many different methods: ultrasound scanning of the uterus and developing foal (a method similar to that used by doctors for pregnant women); an internal examination when the vet feels the developing structures directly through the wall of the mare's rectum (back passage); and urine or blood testing.

All these methods are used at different stages of pregnancy and the vet is the best judge of which is most suitable for a particular mare.

Inside the mare

After conception, the fertilized egg becomes attached to the lining of the mare's **uterus** (womb), where the process of development begins.

The egg divides, first into two cells, then four, then eight, 16 and so on. At first a ball of cells forms and this develops into a hollow sphere. Gradually the shape changes as the body of the foal grows and its internal organs start to form.

A little later on the **membranes** form and **fluid** surrounds the foal for protection. Also, the **placenta** develops. This is the structure which links the foal to the mother's uterus and supplies food and oxygen to the foal via the **umbilical cord**.

The foal's blood also contains waste products from its own body. These are transferred to the mother's blood and taken away in her bloodstream to be expelled from her body.

▲ **By the last few weeks** it usually becomes obvious that the mare is pregnant.

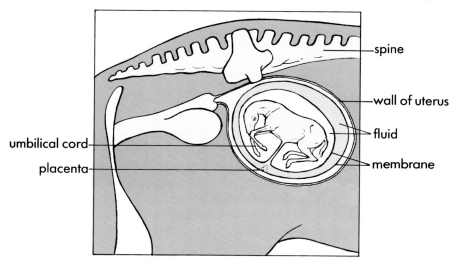

► **Diagrammatic view** of the position of the womb and the developing foal.

The stages of development

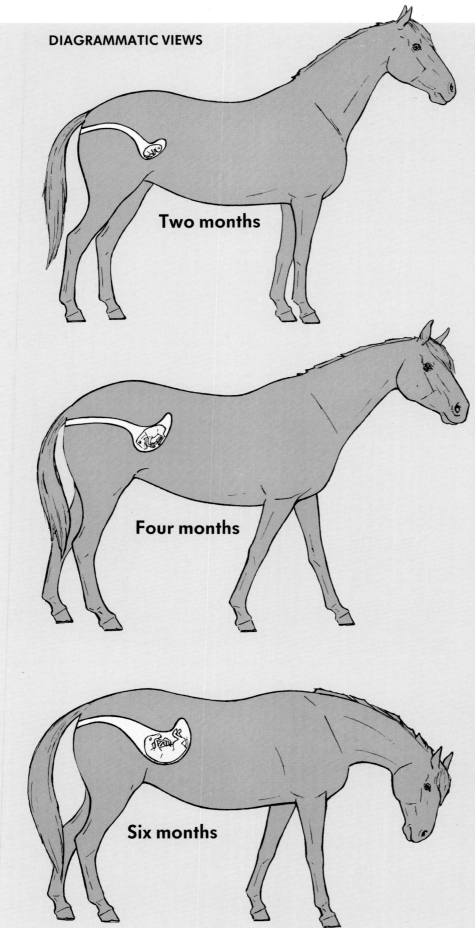

Two months

Four months

Six months

In the first stages, the foal – known as the embryo at this stage – has little recognizable shape.

By 20 days after conception there are already millions of cells and the shape of the legs and head can be seen, although the embryo is only 2cm (about ¾in) long.

Once the limbs and internal organs have started to develop the tiny foal is called a foetus and this name applies up until birth.

At two months the foetus is clearly recognizable as a tiny horse and measures between 5 and 7cm (2–2½in) from head to tail. By three months the hooves have developed and the body is between 7 and 14cm (2½–5½in) long.

At four months hair begins to grow on the lips. Meanwhile the placenta develops and the umbilical cord forms. The foal's body is connected to the placenta by the umbilical cord. Blood circulates around the foal's body and then passes down the blood vessels in the umbilical cord to the placenta. Here it comes into contact with the mother's blood, picking up food and oxygen.

It is now possible to see the earliest change in the mare's waistline.

At six months, when the foal is 30–60cm (12–24in) long, small hairs are developing on the nostrils, the eyelashes and the eyebrows. At seven months the tail is beginning to form. A change in the mare's shape may be fairly obvious. However, the mare's behaviour can still be quite normal, showing no signs of pregnancy.

At eight months the foetus measures from 50–80cm (20–32in) and the mane is starting to form. The outer part of the ear develops and the limbs take shape.

By the tenth month the foal has reached about 60–90cm (24–36in) long and the body, except the abdomen and between the thighs, is covered with a thin layer of short hairs.

In the last stages of pregnancy the foal weighs between 30 and 60kg (66–132lbs) and is between 75 and 145cm (30–60in) long. Just before birth the foal moves into the birth position.

The pregnant mare

In many cases it is only in the last few weeks of pregnancy that the mare starts to get rather restless, often lying down and getting up again, seeming uneasy or being difficult with other horses. In these final weeks the mare must have plenty of peace and quiet and be kept away from horses which may bully her.

Light exercise is quite alright after the first six weeks of pregnancy, but the mare should be allowed to rest from seven months onward.

During pregnancy keep an eye open for changes in the mare's behaviour which can't be explained, and watch for loss of appetite or alteration in her general condition. Also, look for signs of colic and, in particular, for discharge from the mare's vulva.

If anything is worrying about the pregnancy call the vet. Even if nothing is wrong it is best to be reassured that the mare's pregnancy is progressing normally.

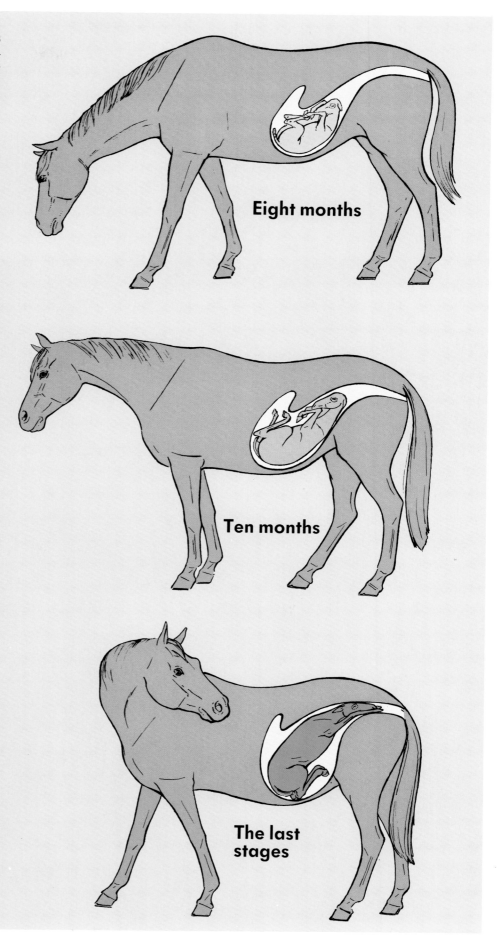

Eight months

Ten months

The last stages

The birth of a foal

A foal comes into the world very quickly once the process of birth begins and there are rarely any problems. However, it's important to have professional help quickly available in case of difficulties.

Before birth begins

Some mares show no sign that they are about to foal, but in most cases the udder starts to enlarge one or two weeks before birth. The mare's quarters may also begin to dip around the same time.

About five days before foaling the mare's teats fill with fluid and about three days before the birth the teats 'wax up' (they become coated in flakes of waxy material). Milk dripping from the teats is a sign that the foal is likely to arrive in the next 24 hours.

As well as these visible signs, tests can be carried out on a milk sample (from about ten days before the foal is due) to predict the time of the birth.

The stages of labour

The first stage of labour (the process of giving birth) varies. A mare in a field with other horses leaves the group and finds a corner of her own. A mare in a stable walks or trots around the box and

► **Foals are well developed** at birth compared with many other mammals. They are soon able to follow their mothers around, staying close by. This mare keeps a close eye on her foal as it rests.

may roll, sweat and start to look at her abdomen. Sometimes this sort of behaviour is only a false alarm and it may happen a week or more before the actual birth.

The birth – the second stage of labour – is generally quick. There is little reason for people to take part in the process. However, any attempts to help the mare should be made with great care in case she kicks or rolls.

The birth process begins with the escape of the fluid which surrounds the foal in the womb. This is known as the 'waters breaking' and there may be up to a gallon (3.8 litres) of fluid.

Once the fluid has escaped, the foal must be delivered quickly – and within no more than three hours – or it will almost certainly die. The mare probably lies down for this part of labour and the foal's forelegs should appear within 20 minutes after her waters break. If this does not happen, and certainly if the hindlegs come first, call the vet.

The foal should be born from five to 30 minutes after the forelegs have appeared. It generally comes into the world covered in the amnion (the inner membrane covering it in the womb).

A foal is born

After delivery the foal frees itself from the amnion with a little help from the mother. If the foal appears weak and the membrane is not broken quickly it should be torn way. Any fluid from the foal's mouth and nostrils should be wiped away.

The mother usually licks and nuzzles the foal to dry it but, if she shows no interest in doing so, the task should be performed for her using straw or towels.

The mare gets to her feet within 40 minutes of the birth and, as she does so, the umbilical cord breaks. The placenta, (now called the afterbirth), is usually produced about 60 minutes after foaling. This process is the third stage of labour and is often referred to as 'cleansing'. If the complete afterbirth is not produced within three hours of foaling a vet must remove it from inside the mare.

Most foals are on their feet about one and a half hours after birth and they should take their first drink from the mother's teats within the next hour. This first milk contains a substance called colostrum which passes on antibodies, to protect the foal from infection.

The birth process

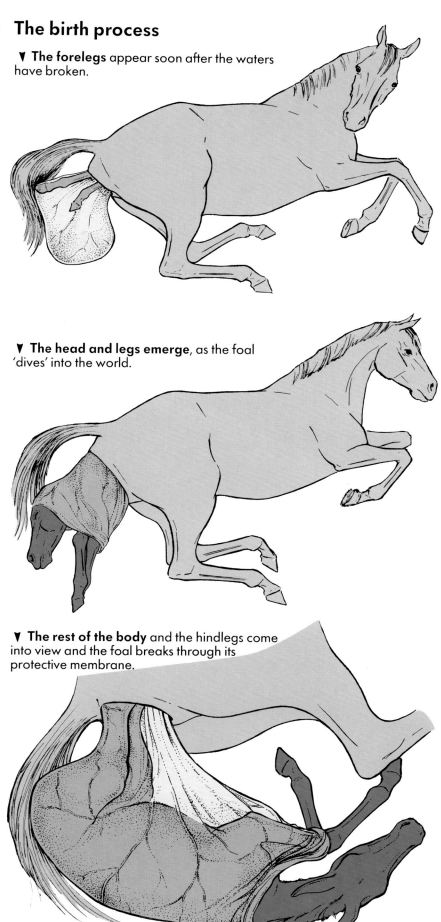

▼ **The forelegs** appear soon after the waters have broken.

▼ **The head and legs emerge**, as the foal 'dives' into the world.

▼ **The rest of the body** and the hindlegs come into view and the foal breaks through its protective membrane.

The first year

Unlike a newborn baby, a foal can stand and walk within a few hours of its birth. After a few days, it can run fast enough to keep up with its mother.

The need to escape

Nowadays, most horses are domesticated and have no fear of other animals. But, in the wild, they are just one link in nature's food chain and must protect themselves against predators like wild cats and dogs.

When foals are born their legs are already 90% of their adult length so that youngsters are instantly equipped for speed – and can escape from danger by running away.

Young horses are naturally inquisitive and eager to learn about their surroundings. They enjoy playing and charge around investigating all the new sights and smells and testing the strength of their legs. This helps to build up their muscles but they soon get tired. To make up for all their skittish activity, regular periods of sleep are essential. Plenty of rest helps 'recharge the batteries' and ensures that the foal is healthy and happy.

Rate of growth

For the first five years of life, one year for a horse equals five human years. So a six-month-old foal is at the same stage of development as a two-and-a-half-year-old child.

▼ **Although a foal's body** is relatively small, its legs are almost the same length as its mother's.

The long legs enable the foal to run quickly so that it can keep up with the herd and escape from any potential danger.

◄ **A mare** gets to know her foal just after the birth. A new mother is usually very protective of her foal and, for the first few days, should be given as much peace and quiet as possible.

◄ **Like most youngsters,** foals have bundles of energy. Exercise develops healthy muscles in the legs — which are always a bit wobbly at first!

Unlike humans, however, a foal achieves about three quarters of its total growth in its first year. During the first four weeks, its height increases by about a third. Development slows slightly, then between six and 12 months the foal shoots up again. Its body fills out and its girth measurement increases.

You can estimate the mature height of a foal when it is three months old. Measure in inches from the point of the elbow to the ground. Halve the number of inches and you have the approximate height in hands. So, a foal which measures 28 inches will be about 14 hands high – as long as it doesn't have any setbacks. Foals who are deprived of exercise and good food, particularly during the first month of life, suffer from bad health and never achieve their full potential height or strength.

A hungry youngster looks tired and thin and stays close to its mother, constantly trying to feed. By contrast, a contented foal is well-rounded, has a shiny coat and spends its life feeding, sleeping and, of course, playing!

► **Friendship** is extremely important to ponies. These Welsh pony foals spend much of their time playing and resting together.

The second year

Although growth in yearlings – horses between 12 and 23 months old – is less dramatic than in foals, a one-year-old shows distinct changes in development and behaviour.

Growing up

From the age of one, a horse's body begins to fill out and starts to catch up with its long legs. The hindquarters, which provide drive and power, increase in strength and become more muscular. As this 'engine room' develops, yearlings can canter and gallop at a reasonable speed but still lack the strength and endurance of more mature horses.

In their first autumn, the youngsters lose their fluffy foal coats and the short, soft hair in their manes and tails is replaced by 'proper' hair. This more grown-up appearance can lead to quite dramatic changes and the new coat may be a completely different colour from the old one! A dun foal may, for example, become either bay or brown unless it is a true dun – with black legs, mane and tail and a dark stripe along the backbone. It is also quite common for a chestnut foal to turn grey if it has one grey parent.

▼ **Playing** is a favourite pastime for yearlings. Games are quite competitive and are an indication of fights for dominance in later life.

Although horses are not sexually mature until the age of three, yearlings can serve (mate with) females and get them in foal. So yearlings should always be kept away from mares when turned out in a field.

Competition time

As they play together, yearlings are more boisterous and more competitive than foals. They are weaned from their dams (mothers) and usually have no adult horse among them to keep order: instead, they must establish their own pecking order and decide who is boss!

Croup high

In yearlings, the highest point of the hindquarters — the croup — is usually above the highest point of the forehand — the withers. This conformation (shown by the red line on the right) is called 'croup high', and is normal in youngsters.

The hindquarters develop earlier because, like an engine, they provide the power to drive a horse forward. This makes the yearling look out of proportion for a while.

The withers and croup usually even up at the age of three or four. But in some horses they never catch up. These mounts give their riders the feeling that they are going downhill all the time — not a very pleasant experience!

▲ **The body** begins to fill out and catch up with the long hindlegs, but the face still looks young.

▼ **Yearlings are** still developing their speed, although they may look full of energy. They are not yet strong enough to run for long periods of time.

45

The middle years

A horse is usually fully mature when he is six years old. By then, he has reached his full height and his bones are fully grown and 'hardened'.

Filling out

The main change you'll notice in a horse's appearance is a general filling out of his body. This is because his muscles have developed. He looks bigger and more imposing, but without getting any taller.

His adult life should be long and productive as long as he has been well looked after during his early years.

▼ Filling out: As the horse gets older and does more work, his body becomes broader and more muscular. This makes him seem larger even though he's already reached his full adult height.

Strength and stamina

The speed a horse builds up as a youngster reaches its greatest point between the years of two and six. From then on, his actual speed lessens but is replaced by increased strength and stamina.

He *gets* fit more quickly than a young or old horse and *stays* fit longer without needing a rest or holiday.

The prime of life

A horse's 'teenage' years, in human terms, are from three to five. After he is six years old, you can reckon that one

year to us equals three to a horse. So, from six to 14, he's at roughly the same stage as a person of 18 to 45.

A horse is at his peak, in the prime of life, between eight and 12-14. These middle years are often a horse's healthiest. He is no longer plagued so much by the health problems of the young – teething, strangles, jarred limbs, warts, breathing diseases. But he hasn't yet succumbed to the disorders of the elderly either.

Provided his work is sensibly balanced, it is difficult to overburden a fit, healthy and well-cared-for horse at this time of life.

Fully formed

Once the word 'teen' appears in a horse's age, some people feel he is getting past his best. But many horses continue to work eagerly and productively even after the age of 14.

Technically, a horse is said to be 'aged' when he is eight years old. Aged in this sense doesn't necessarily mean old, just that you can no longer tell his age accurately.

At the age of eight, a horse's character is fully developed and he knows about the world. His outlook on life – whether sensible, calm and wise or nervous, excitable and scatty – is unlikely to change much now.

▲ **Speed gives way** to strength and stamina; a horse can work harder now than at any other time in his life.

◄ **Worldly wise:** By the age of eight, a horse has learnt a lot about life, and his character is formed.

▼ **Horses** in the prime of life are usually at their healthiest, free of the problems of the young and old.

The last years

Physically, horses in their 20's are past their best, but mentally they are often in better shape than their younger counterparts.

Schoolmasters

For many purposes, older horses are better than younger ones: they are experienced and usually sensible and unruffled by any situation.

They can make excellent 'schoolmaster' animals, being patient and steady enough for beginners to learn to ride on them. They show young horses the ropes when out hacking, giving a lead over tricky places and in traffic. And, when travelling, they have a calming influence on ponies who are nervous about being boxed.

Growing old

The average lifespan for a horse is 25 years, although it has been known for them to live much longer than this. A Cleveland cross-breed called 'Old Billy', born in 1760, is said to have lived to the remarkable age of 62!

Ponies tend to live longer than horses. A 20-year old pony is about equal to a 70-year old human, a 30-year old pony to a 100-year old human.

▼ **Just because a** horse gets old doesn't mean you can't ride him any more. Indeed, regular (almost daily), steady exercise is much better for him than little or no work.

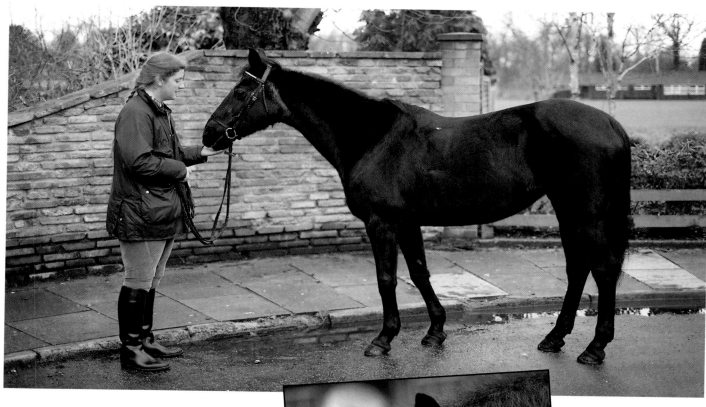

Older horses cannot work as hard or for as long as young ones. But regular, light exercise keeps them healthier than occasional work or none at all.

Like all old animals, horses feel their age sooner or later. They become slower and stiffer as their joints lose mobility, and their limbs and body in general lose their youthful suppleness. Because of this it becomes increasingly difficult for horses to lie down and stand up again, so they often prefer to stand while resting.

Body matters

Older horses are likely to suffer from disorders such as arthritis and rheumatism, and the circulation and digestion begin to deteriorate. As the teeth begin to wear down, old horses commonly suffer from dental problems.

The horse's outward appearance also changes. Some old horses start to lose weight. Careful management of work and feeding is required to prevent them from losing condition, especially in the winter, when they feel the cold more.

The back may sink down a little, and the legs bend slightly forward at the knees and sink lower at the fetlocks.

The colour of the coat can change – for example, a grey pony lightens with age. Other colours may produce grey hairs in the coat, particularly on the head – giving a grizzled, slightly 'dusty' look.

▲ **Slightly bent knees** are a common feature of old age, as the leg joints stiffen up.

◄ **Just like humans,** some horses go grey as they get older.

▼ **It is often hard** to tell if a pony is old just by looking at him. A hollow (dipped) back is a good clue.

2 Getting started

Fitting tack

▼ **The saddle** must have a rider in it before the saddler sees how it fits the pony. It must also suit you, even when you change position for jumping (inset).

The basic tack you need when you've just bought a pony is a saddle, with girth, stirrup leathers and irons, a simple bridle, probably with a snaffle bit, and a headcollar.

General-purpose saddle

There are various sorts of saddles for specialized equestrian disciplines such as show jumping, dressage, showing, long-distance riding and racing. But the most useful to begin with is a general-purpose saddle.

These types are designed so that you can comfortably use different lengths of stirrup leather because the flap, on which your leg rests, extends slightly toward the shoulder.

When you raise your stirrups for jumping your knee comes forward, so you need a saddle which lets your leg move without your knee going off the flap. However, when your stirrups are the normal length for flatwork, there must be enough flap *behind* your leg.

Fitting the saddle

To check how it fits, the saddle must be on the horse with a rider on his back and someone experienced to hand. If the saddle does not fit your pony properly, it could make him very sore from pressure or rubbing.

Once you are in the saddle, you should be able to fit the width of your hand in front of your body without it going off the saddle, and the same at the back. The flap should allow for your different leg positions.

With the pommel in its normal position just over the back part of the withers, the cantle must be on the pony's back and not extending on to his

There should be no pressure points when you lean backward . . .

. . . or forward.

loin and kidney area. As for width, the saddle must not slip and rock from side to side (too wide) or pinch his withers and seem to perch above them (too narrow). You should just be able to slide the flat of your fingers under the saddle at the front on each side.

Ask your pony's heaviest rider to sit in the saddle, and ride around for about 15 minutes. This lets it settle on to the pony's back. You should now be able to fit three, and preferably four, fingers sideways between the withers and the pommel, and the cantle and backbone.

Looking down the gullet (from cantle to pommel) when the rider is mounted, you must be able to see a clear

PROBLEM CONFORMATION

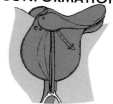

Ponies with a good deal of Thoroughbred blood often have high withers which can make saddle-fitting a problem. In such cases, you may need to buy a saddle with a 'cut-back head'. The pommel is cut away backward to fit round the withers.

Ponies with flat withers and little shape in front, or those who are rather fat, cause the saddle to slip forward. They may need girths which are shaped behind the elbows to avoid chafing.

They may also need a crupper (a loop going under the tail and buckling to the back of the saddle) to hold the saddle back.

You should be able to fit a hand's width behind and in front of you.

The pommel must not press on or pinch the withers.

There must be a tunnel of daylight along the pony's backbone.

tunnel of daylight all the way down the pony's backbone. The tunnel should still be there when the rider leans forward and back. It is most important that the saddle does not press anywhere at all along the backbone.

The stuffing should be smoothly distributed inside the seat panels (the two built-in pads on the underside of the saddle), so that there is even pressure on the pony's back.

The saddle must be well balanced. You should be able to sit in the deepest part of the seat – the centre. It should not tip you forward or let you slide back when the pony moves.

Some saddles with high cantles are tricky to judge, and you may need your instructor to advise you, particularly if the saddle seems strange and uncomfortable at first.

The bridle

The bridle should fit so you can easily slide a finger under it all over the pony's head. If it is too tight, it will be most uncomfortable and could cause soreness.

The browband is not adjustable so you must get the right size. Most small ponies take pony-size and those of 14.2 hands high upward take cob size, but much depends on whether or not your pony has a big head! The browband should allow the headpiece to lie comfortably behind the ears without pulling it into the base of the ears; the browband itself should lie just below the base of

SECOND-
HAND TACK

It is much better to buy good quality used tack than poorer quality new tack for the same price. The poorer new tack will not last as long, does not have a high re-sale value and may be dangerous. Most reputable saddlers stock good secondhand tack.

Do not buy used tack at a tack auction unless you have someone very knowledgeable with you.

Numnahs

A numnah (saddle pad) is useful for absorbing sweat (unless it is nylon) and for giving the pony a softer, more comfortable feel on his back. However, it is not essential for your starting-off tack, and a thick numnah is not an excuse to use a badly fitting saddle. Numnahs do not remove pressure; they only lessen it.

If you do buy one, make certain you pull it up fully into the saddle gullet all the way along when saddling up. You should be able to pass your whip right down the pony's back from pommel to cantle. If the numnah is flat on the back, the saddle pushes it down further. Your weight causes quite firm pressure on the back, particularly the withers, and the pad can make your pony very sore.

Make sure, too, that the numnah is not creased or tucked up anywhere beneath the saddle; this creates uneven pressure and more soreness. The numnah should also be cleaned regularly to prevent chafing.

the ears so it does not cut into them. It should not be so long, however, that it flops about.

The other parts of the bridle are adjustable with buckles. You should be able to fit the width of four fingers between the throat-lash and the pony's round jawbones.

The bit itself should show about 7mm (¼in) each side of the pony's mouth. If it is wider it slides about and does not act properly or evenly; if it is narrower it pinches.

Adjust the bridle cheekpieces so that the bit *just* wrinkles the corners of the pony's mouth. If the bit is too low it could bang on his teeth or make it possible for him to get his tongue over the mouthpiece and evade its action; if it is too high it is uncomfortable and could make his lips sore at the corners.

With a well-schooled pony who goes nicely, you do not *have* to have a noseband. A plain cavesson noseband makes a pony look 'dressed', but do not buy any other kind unless your instructor advises it.

The headcollar

A headcollar is better than a rope or web halter, which is not as practical,

Oiling

Before using leather tack for the first time, give it extra protection by oiling or dressing it. You can use neatsfoot oil or a branded, lanolin-based leather dressing, available from hardware stores.

Give two *thin* coats. Pour the dressing into a bowl or saucer and use a paintbrush about 2.5cm (1in) wide. Pay particular attention to the underside of your bridle, saddle flaps, girth tabs and stirrup leathers as these are the most absorbent. Don't over-oil or you'll make everything slimy. Re-dress the tack if it gets very wet so it remains in good condition and does not lose its suppleness.

strong or easy to use. The headcollar can be leather, or cotton or nylon webbing. The noseband is all in one with the rest.

The basic fit is the same as for bridles. You should be able to get the width of three fingers between the noseband and the pony's nose (most are much too big and loose). The noseband should come midway between the corners of the lips and the sharp face bones so it doesn't rub. If it is lower the pony might be able to push it off.

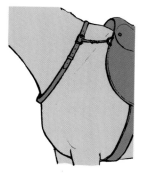

NECK STRAP
A neck strap is a useful piece of tack, even if you aren't a beginner. You can buy the leather 'collar', which fits round the base of your pony's neck and fastens with two leather loops to the front D-rings of the saddle.

Alternatively, you can improvise with a stirrup leather and binder twine. Buckle the leather round the pony's neck and put one loop of binder twine through the buckle. Attach this to the D-ring to stop the buckle slipping down to the breast and perhaps cutting into the pony.

On the opposite side, tie binder twine to the other D-ring and thread it through a hole in the stirrup leather to secure it.

◄ **A well-fitting** bridle leaves room for you to slide a finger under every part, and the width of four fingers between the throat-lash and the pony's jawbones.

Snaffle bits

The snaffle is usually thought of as the simplest and mildest bit. But in fact the name 'snaffle' covers a whole family of bits, which vary in their action on the pony's mouth. All, however, consist of a mouthpiece with rings at each end to which the reins and cheekpieces are attached.

How snaffles work

When correctly fitted, snaffles operate by exerting pressure on the bars of the pony's mouth – his gums, across the portion of the mouth where the bit rests – and on the corners of his lips. You can see this working to some extent if you stand alongside a pony's head while his

➤ **An egg-butt snaffle** is one of the kindest bits you can use. The rings are fixed so your pony's mouth does not get pinched, while the wide mouthpieces are comfortable for him. It is an ideal everyday bit.

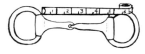

MEASURING UP

Snaffle bits are measured in inches between the two rings. As a rough guide, ponies usually take a 5in (12cm) jointed bit size, and a 4½in (11cm) unjointed mouthpiece, but ask an expert to help you fit a new bit.

DID YOU KNOW?

The jointed snaffle is believed to be one of the first bits invented for riding in prehistoric times.

Archaeologists have found, preserved in peat bogs, pony-sized bits thousands of years old. They are almost identical to the jointed snaffles ponies wear today.

rider gives rein aids.

Inside the pony's mouth, the snaffle also puts pressure on the pony's tongue. How much pressure depends on the kind of snaffle used. Overall, the effect is to bring the pony's head up and in, helping you to regulate his pace, steer and stop him. Whatever bit you use, however, your body and legs should be doing most of the work of controlling the pony!

Kinds of snaffle

The mildest form of snaffle has a thick, unjointed, gently curved mouthpiece (often known as mullen mouth) made of rubber.

▼ **Many ponies** are bitted with a loose-ring, plain, jointed snaffle. It is simple and easy to use. The rings are rounded to stop them rubbing the pony's face.

The rubber or hardened rubber (vulcanite) makes it even easier on the pony's mouth. This is a good bit for a young pony, or for one with a tender, sensitive mouth; a pony which fidgets and gets upset in a stronger bit often goes quietly in a rubber snaffle.

The plain, jointed snaffle, usually made of uncovered metal, has a two-part mouthpiece with a joint in the middle. This gives the bit a 'nutcracker' action, with more pressure on the pony's tongue. It allows the rider greater control – in theory, at least!

Some snaffles are more severe than others. Harsher types may have a twisted, rather than a plain, jointed mouthpiece, or a series of rollers inside or fitted round the mouthpiece. Otherwise there may be two thin mouthpieces, each with a separate joint at a different point across the mouth, for a double nutcracker effect.

Harsher snaffles are used for ponies that 'lean' on your hands, pull or are hard to stop and steer. They are not beginners' bits! They should be bought, fitted in ponies' mouths, and used only with expert supervision.

The snaffle rings

The rings on a snaffle stop the bit sliding through the mouth. They may be loose – fitted through holes in each outer (butt) end of the mouthpiece – or fixed, as in the popular, eggbutt snaffle. The rings, however, can move sideways even with a fixed-ring snaffle.

Older, loose-ring snaffles usually had wide, flat rings. Nowadays, the rings are often rounded as these are less likely to rub the pony's face. And, as they only need small holes in the butts of the mouthpiece, there is less risk of pinching the pony's lips.

Snaffle bits in old-fashioned racing prints often had long 'cheeks' (vertical strips) set between mouthpiece and ring. These are a steering aid, as the cheek applies pressure against the side of the horse's face.

Buying the right bit

Snaffles today are usually made in stainless steel or vulcanite. They come in half-inch sizes. For safety and comfort, the mouthpiece of the bit must be the right width. If it is too narrow, it pinches the pony's lips; if it is too wide, the bit slips about in the mouth.

It's easy when you are buying a new snaffle for your pony, and know his old bit is the right fitting; just measure across the mouthpiece. If you are not sure, ask an expert to help, or explain your problem to the saddler. From your pony's size and breeding, he probably knows the bit size you need. Then have your expert make sure that the bit is fitted correctly on to the bridle and in the pony's mouth.

A bit can be fitted on to the bridle and reins with buckles or stud billets (like a hook and eye they are neat, but less easy to undo). It can be sewn permanently into place, although this is more appropriate for a showing bridle.

Whatever you choose, clean the bridle and bit thoroughly and regularly. Check for worn places on fastenings, straps, rings and mouthpiece – a bridle or bit that breaks is a frightening experience. Don't ask your pony to wear a rough, rusty old bit, or one covered with stale froth and grass – but don't give him a mouthful of metal polish, either!

▼ **The snaffle** is a versatile bit that can be used successfully to a fairly high standard of riding. It is only when you reach an advanced level of dressage work or serious showing that you need more precision for perfect collection and control.

Popular types of snaffle

For everyday riding — hacking, hunting, competition work or jumping — there is almost sure to be at least one among the family of snaffle bits which suits you and your pony.

Always ask an expert to help you fit the bit and advise you on what kind to choose. The snaffles shown here are the types most commonly found.

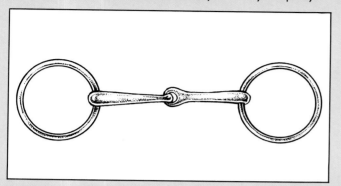

Plain, jointed snaffle

When you start riding, the pony you learn on is often bitted with the simplest bit, the plain, jointed snaffle. Usually made of stainless steel, it has two rounded bars linked in the centre, with rings at either end. The central join gives you more control than a straight bar.

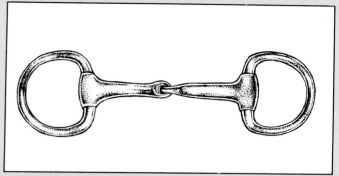

Eggbutt snaffle

Unlike the plain, jointed snaffle, the eggbutt snaffle has fixed rings. These help stop the rings sliding and pinching the pony's lips. It is a popular bit that suits many ponies, and is a good choice for a first buy.

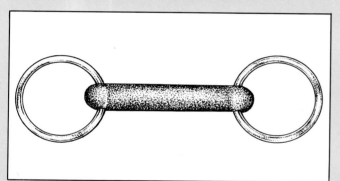

Unjointed, rubber snaffle

This is the mildest type of snaffle and it is good for young or very sensitive ponies that are nervous of bits. The rubber or hardened rubber (vulcanite) has a metal core for safety.

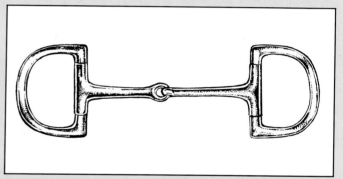

D-ring snaffle

Derived from cheek snaffles, the D-ring snaffle is sometimes used for racehorses. The straight side of the D, set against the horse's face, acts as a mini-cheek to help with steering. It is also an extra safeguard against the bit pinching the lips or slipping through the mouth.

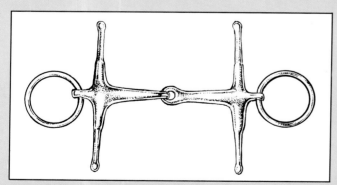

Fulmer cheek snaffle

So called from a famous English riding school where its use was brought to a fine art, this cheek snaffle has loose rings separate from the cheeks. Many ponies go well in this mild bit. It needs retaining straps for the top cheeks, attached to the bridle, to keep the bit in place.

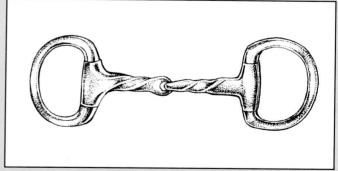

Twisted snaffle

This is a strong bit because the twisted mouthpiece is severe in action. It should only be used in expert hands and on a pony with a hard mouth. It can either have loose rings or fixed ones.

Saddling up

When you have built up your confidence by being around ponies and practising the basic paces, it's time to learn about tacking up – putting on the saddle and bridle.

Safety first

At the riding school, each pony has his own tack which fits well and comfortably (for both horse and rider) and is maintained in clean condition. No other pony uses his saddle and bridle.

Properly fitted tack is essential. Ill-fitting equipment can rub, causing sores which may become infected, harming the pony and keeping him off work until he's healed. Also, it is uncomfortable and irritating for the pony and potentially dangerous for you, as he may be frustrated into rearing or bolting as he

EGGBUTT SNAFFLE
A jointed eggbutt snaffle is one of the mildest forms of bit. It's likely that this will be the bit you use when you start to ride.

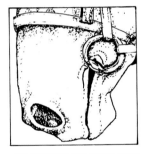

CHECKING THE BIT
When you've placed the bit inside the pony's mouth and before you fasten the buckles up, check that the bit fits correctly. The pony's mouth should be wrinkling a little at the corners.

► **Tacking up a pony** on your own makes you more independent and confident around the stables.

tries to get rid of the discomfort.

Hard, dry, uncared-for leather is a problem for the same reasons, and because it may break. If you help to clean the tack, check the leather for wear and the stitching for signs of weakness. Caring for tack is a basic safety precaution in riding. Well-fitting, regularly maintained tack is safe; anything else is not.

How to prepare

It's a good idea if a more experienced person stands by during your first attempt to tack up. You'll be concentrating on keeping control of the pony while juggling with saddle and bridle. You can prepare by being familiar with what the bridle looks like when it is on the pony. If you have ever cleaned the tack you'll be used to the various parts.

When you collect the bridle from the tack room you may find that the throatlash has been crossed over the front of the bridle with the reins looped over it at the back. When you undo the throatlash the reins will drop down quite easily. The noseband may also be outside the cheekpieces and this should be placed inside before putting the bridle on the pony.

Approaching the pony

When you leave the tack room you should have with you bridle, saddle – complete with stirrup leathers, irons and girth – plus headcollar and rope (this may be outside the pony's box).

Once at the stable, carefully put the tack down. Don't rest the saddle on the stable door. It may crash to the ground and it puts strain on the stable door hinges.

Walk confidently into the stable and bolt the door behind you. Standing on the near side, put the headcollar on the pony. Decide where you are going to tack up and secure him there with a quick-release knot. If you saddle up in the stable, remember to bolt the door behind you as you go in and out to pick up the tack.

Positioning the saddle

The saddle should sit comfortably just behind the withers. With fat, or naturally round ponies, this point might be difficult to distinguish, but there is usually a dip behind the withers.

Stand on the near side. With your left hand on the pommel and your right hand on the cantle, lift the saddle. Make sure the girth is over the seat of the ➤

▼ **Placing the saddle** has to be done carefully. By sliding it back into position from the withers, the hairs lie flat under the saddle and the pony feels comfortable.

Fitting the bridle

1 Stand on the pony's near side and refasten the headcollar round his neck so he remains secure.

2 Place the reins over his neck. Hold the bridle in your right hand and use your left hand to guide the bit in.

3 Once the bit is positioned, put the headpiece on — guide it over the pony's ears until it rests on the poll.

4 Before you fasten any straps up, check that the bit looks comfortable in the pony's mouth and that it is above the tongue. Then you can buckle up the throat-lash fairly loosely.

5 Fasten the noseband so that it fits snugly; remember it fits inside the cheekpieces. Check that the noseband and browband are level.

6 Pull the forelock out from under the browband and any mane from under the headpiece. Loop your arm through the rein nearest to you while you remove the headcollar. The pony is now fully tacked up.

Testing the fit

▲ **The noseband** fits properly if there is space for one finger's width.

▲ **The throat-lash** should be four fingers' width away from the pony's jaw.

! TAKING THE BIT
● Most ponies open their mouths ready to take the bit, but the odd one is more reluctant. If you are having problems getting the bit in, just slide your thumb — on the hand supporting the bit — into the side of the pony's mouth, two thirds of the way back. Here, a little before the corner of his mouth, he hasn't any teeth so you won't get nipped!

saddle. Place the saddle a little further up the withers than you would want to sit. Then just slide the saddle down until it comes to rest naturally on the pony's back. This ensures that the hair underneath lies flat.

The pommel and cantle should appear about level when the saddle is in the correct position. If it is not in the right place, your own position will be wrong. This makes riding uncomfortable and makes your aids ineffective.

When the saddle is correctly placed, walk around the front of the pony and drop the girth down, making sure the girth straps are not twisted. As you do this, try to keep a hand on the saddle for as long as possible. Come back again to the near side, reach underneath the pony for the girth and do it up gently. Keep the girth fairly loose at first and tighten it before you get on.

The bridle and the bit

If the bridle belongs to the pony it will already be adjusted correctly so you won't have to worry about that the first time. However, checking that the bridle looks about the right size is a good habit to acquire. Hold the bridle alongside the pony's face, sideways on, to make sure the bit will lie in the correct position in his mouth.

There are various methods of saddling up, but the basics remain the same. Watch other people tacking up and learn from them, but always maintain high safety standards and don't cut corners.

Alternative tack

Drop nosebands are quite common. They are used on headstrong ponies to increase the rider's control. Instead of fastening above the level of the bit, the drop noseband passes underneath the bit rings, fastening in the chin groove. It should not 'droop' too low on the nose or it interferes with the pony's breathing. But it must be tight enough to stop the pony from opening his mouth, without pinching him.

Cruppers go under the tail and fasten on to the saddle. They are used for small, round ponies to stop the saddle slipping forward. They are often lined with towelling to prevent rubbing. If the pony wears a crupper, this will already be attached to the back of the saddle, so simply pass the tail through the loop until the crupper rests at the top of the dock.

Removing the pony's tack

An important aspect of learning to ride is knowing what to do when a ride has finished. The pony must be made comfortable and the tack removed and stored safely.

The end of the ride

At the end of a lesson always make sure the pony arrives at his stable cool and relaxed. Make the transition from walk to halt; when the pony is standing still give him a pat on the neck to thank him. Still mounted, loosen your girth one or two holes.

Dismount and then take the reins over the pony's head. Keep your arm looped through the reins so you still have control.

The stirrups

Run the stirrups up the stirrup leathers so they are secure and not flapping and banging against the pony's sides: take the top of the stirrup leather into one hand to do this.

With your other hand run the stirrup iron up the underneath leather until it reaches the buckle end of the leather. Pass the remaining leather through the stirrup iron so that it is held in place and cannot slip back down.

Removing the saddle

Unbuckle the girth on the left side of the pony and lay it over the top of the seat. Be careful not to let the buckles of the girth bang against the saddle or scratch the leather.

With your left hand on the pommel (front of the saddle) and your right on the cantle (back of the saddle), lift the saddle off the pony's back and carefully put it on the ground. Lean it against the stable wall with the pommel on the ground and the cantle balanced against a wall so that the saddle cannot possibly fall over.

Never hang the saddle on the stable door as it could easily fall to the ground and be damaged. Even better than standing the saddle on the ground is having a small foldaway saddle rack just outside the stable door for the saddle to rest on until you have removed the bridle.

◄ **Always handle tack with care.** Prop the saddle against a wall while you take the bridle off. Never balance a saddle on the stable door where it could easily tip off and be damaged.

How to take off the saddle

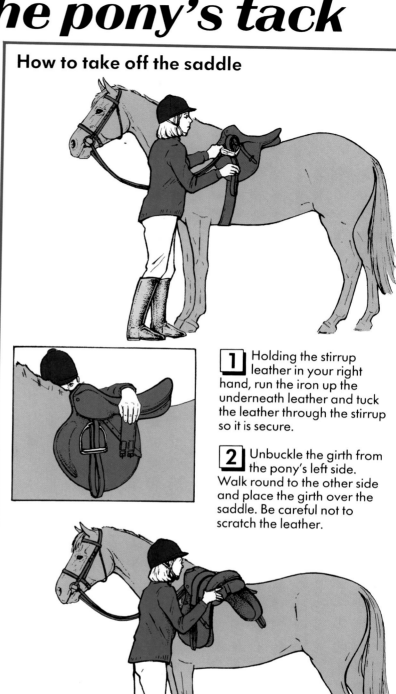

1 Holding the stirrup leather in your right hand, run the iron up the underneath leather and tuck the leather through the stirrup so it is secure.

2 Unbuckle the girth from the pony's left side. Walk round to the other side and place the girth over the saddle. Be careful not to scratch the leather.

3 Remove the saddle by placing your left hand on the pommel (front) and your right hand on the cantle (back) and lifting it off gently.

4 Put the saddle on the ground, pommel down, and with the cantle resting against a wall, until you can store it properly.

SADDLE HORSE
The safest place to store a saddle is on a rack specially designed for the purpose.

Removing the bridle

Before taking the bridle off, strap a headcollar round the pony's neck. This way you always have control.

To remove the bridle, undo the noseband and the throat-lash. Lift the headpiece and reins together over the pony's ears. If you can, use one hand to catch the bit as the bridle comes off.

Now you can fit the headcollar. Place the noseband over the pony's muzzle. With your right hand put the headpiece over his poll and just behind his ears. Do up the cheekpiece, allowing about four fingers' width between it and the pony. Tie him up with a quick-release knot while you put the tack away.

Carrying the tack

Always carry the tack properly to avoid scratching the leather or, worse, breaking the saddle.

Hold the bridle by the headpiece together with the reins in your left hand. If you're small, try not to let the reins drag along the ground. If you are tall you won't have difficulty with this – you can carry the bridle in your left hand at waist or shoulder level.

There are two ways to carry the saddle. One is on your right arm with the pommel in the crook of your elbow, the bridle remaining in your left hand.

The second method is easier if you are small. Put the headpiece of the bridle

BRIDLE PARTS

headpiece

throat-lash

browband

noseband

bit

cheekpiece

How to take off the bridle

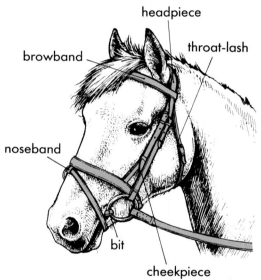

1 Strap the headcollar around the pony's neck before taking off the bridle and check it's not too tight.

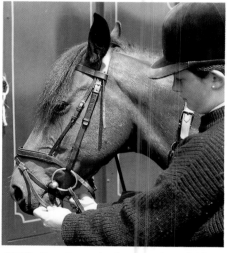

2 Gently undo the noseband. This pony is wearing a noseband called a flash.

3 Once the noseband is undone, unstrap the throat-lash. Then you can take the bridle off.

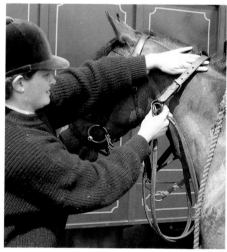

4 Gently slip the headpiece and reins over his head. The bit will drop from his mouth as you do this.

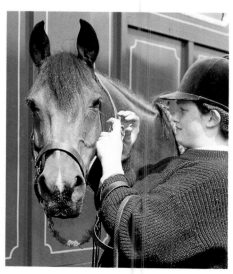

5 Fit the headcollar properly. When you do up the cheekpiece, allow about four fingers' width.

with the reins on to your left shoulder. This leaves both of your hands free to carry the saddle. The left hand holds the pommel, the right hand the cantle.

Storing the tack

Keep the tack in a safe place. At riding schools there is usually a special room called a tack room where you find hooks for the bridles and saddle racks to put the saddles on. If you have your own pony you will probably keep your saddlery at home. The bridle should be hung up and the saddle put on a saddle rack or a specially made rack called a saddle horse. If this isn't possible, store the saddle somewhere safe.

▲ **Loop the reins** through the throatlash, so they don't fall to the ground and get dirty.

◄ **Carry the bridle** on your left shoulder – the reins don't trail and you can hold the saddle in both hands.

Tack tips

☐ Always take care of your saddlery and keep it clean.
☐ Never drop your saddle or bridle on the ground — it may crack the bit and will certainly damage the saddle.
☐ Never lead your pony with his stirrups dangling. They may bang his sides and hurt him.
☐ Always approach your pony from in front and speak to him so that he knows you are there.
☐ Never shout or hurry when moving in the stable, as you can frighten a pony and he may injure himself.
☐ Always bring your pony in cool from exercise and lead him to his stable.
☐ Never ride your pony into his stable: the door is too low.
☐ If you ride at a school, offer to help put the pony away.

Cleaning the tack

Dry, cracked tack is uncomfortable for the pony and dangerous for the rider. Cleaning it regularly keeps the leather supple and strong.

What you need

To clean the tack, you need a bucket of clean, lukewarm water; a bar of saddle soap (from a saddler's or leather store); and two thinnish sponges. One is for washing and one for soaping. Never mix them up or both become useless. Using different colours helps to keep them separate.

Other useful items are a matchstick for poking excess soap out of buckle holes; a coin or blunt knife for removing lumps of grease; and a chamois (pronounced *shammy*) leather – imitation is fine – for drying the leatherwork.

For polishing the stirrups, buckles and bit rings or cheeks, you need some

▼ **Ideally, after every use** you should clean the tack. Rest the saddle on your knee if you don't have a saddle horse.

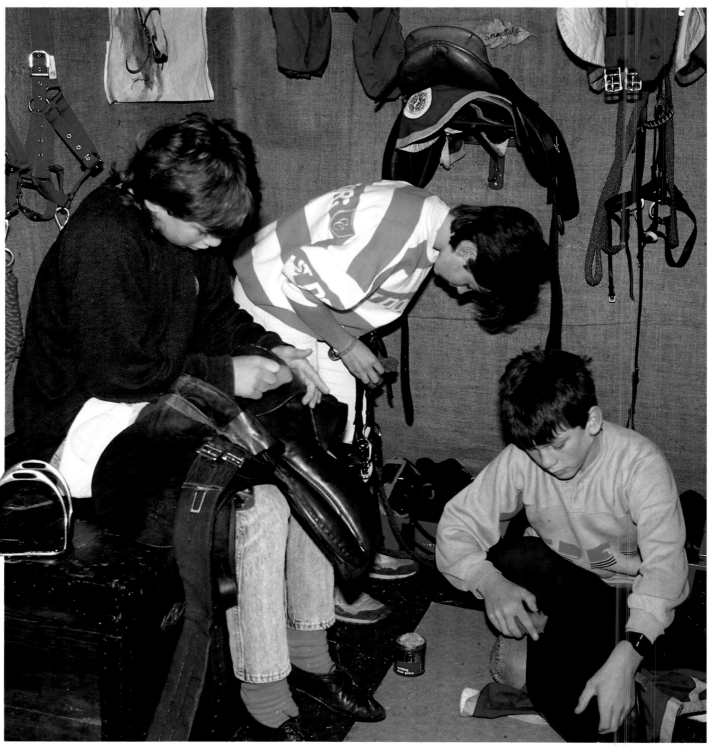

metal polish and two cloths: one for applying and one for bringing up the shine. A stable rubber (or old tea towel) is handy for holding polished metalwork so you don't fingermark it.

Wash and dry the metal every time you clean the tack and polish it about once a month or before special occasions. Never put polish on the mouthpiece and clean off any that spills on to the leather.

You'll find it easier to clean the tack if you have a bridle hook suspended from the ceiling (but mind your head!) or a wall bracket, so you can hang up the bridle, and a saddle horse to rest your saddle on.

Try to clean tack after each use. If you don't have time, at least damp-sponge the underside, because the chemicals in sweat can rot leather.

How to clean the saddle

Strip the saddle – remove the girth and the stirrup leathers – and take the stirrup irons off their leathers.

Dampen the washing sponge, and wipe off the mud. Rinse the sponge and squeeze it out, then firmly rub off grease. If little lumps of black grease (called 'jockeys') cling, gently scrape them off with a handful of horse hair, a coin or blunt knife. Leave the saddle to dry or rub it with the chamois, and wash the stirrup leathers.

Never dunk your saddle in water to wash it. The panel stuffing could shrink and become hard and lumpy, altering the fit and making it uncomfortable. If your tack is very greasy, use warm – not hot – water with two or three drops – not squirts – of washing-up liquid. And never dry wet leather by artificial heat or in direct sunlight as it might crack.

Dip the bar of soap into the water and rub it on the other, soaping, sponge. *Don't* dip the sponge in the water and rub it on the soap as it will be too wet and foamy. The sponge should be barely damp and never rinsed.

Rub soap into the saddle with a circular motion. Pay particular attention underneath the flaps, and to the parts which touch the pony and to the girth straps. Frequently re-soap the sponge. When you've done the saddle, soap the stirrup leathers.

If your girth is leather, clean it the same way. Hang it in a loop by both sets of buckles to dry.

Washing the saddle

1 Start by taking off the girth and girth guards, and the stirrup leathers.

2 Wash the underside carefully, particularly if you don't use a numnah under the saddle.

3 Lift the saddle flap and take the grease off both sides of leather, remembering the straps.

4 Rinse your sponge and squeeze it. Now clean the top of the saddle and round the cantle.

5 Wash the parts you took off the saddle: the stirrup leathers, girth guard and the girth if it is made of leather. For a fabric girth, scrub it with baby soap (which is very pure and so doesn't irritate the pony's skin). Rinse the soap off thoroughly.

Leave the saddle to dry, or rub it with the chamois leather, before soaping it.

bucket of lukewarm water

metal polish

chamois leather

cloth

saddle soap

two sponges

blunt knife

Essential items for cleaning tack are water, two sponges and saddle soap. A knife is useful for scraping off grease; for polishing you need metal polish and some cloths.

OILING TACK

Regularly used tack cleaned with saddle soap stays supple. However, you should use a leather dressing to oil new tack.

After that, you can, if you wish, oil the leather parts that take the greatest strain (usually the straps) about once every three months.

▼ **At Pony Club camp,** you'll find that cleaning tack is a regular task. Your pony can watch you doing all the work while he relaxes with a hay net!

Soaping the saddle

1 Dip the bar of soap into the water. Never dip the *sponge* in water and rub it on the soap, as you will work up far too much lather.

2 Take your second sponge — *not* the one you used for washing. Rub soap on to the sponge, which should be barely damp.

3 Rub soap into the saddle. Pay particular attention to the girth straps as these get a lot of wear from the buckles.

4 Do the girth if it is leather, making sure you work the soap into the individual strands so they are supple and don't rub the pony.

The bridle

It's most thorough to take the bridle to pieces. However, until you are confident that you can put it back together again, you may prefer to keep it in one piece! In this case, move all the buckles a hole or two so that the leather actually touched by metal (which wears and cracks most easily) is properly soaped.

If your bridle is very muddy, do what the army and police often do – dunk it in the bucket to rinse off the mud. But it then needs careful drying and plenty of soap. Preferably clean it on the bridle hook, bracket or table.

Rinse and squeeze out the sponge. Wrap it round each strap and wash off all the grease, most of which will be on the underside. Grip the sponge firmly and run it up and down each strap with one hand, while keeping the leather taut with the other.

Soap the bridle as you did the saddle, but use an up-and-down action. Remember to take extra care over the parts normally touched by metal.

The metalwork

1 Pull the treads out of the stirrup irons and wash the mud off both.

2 When dry, apply the metal polish. A towel on your lap stops you getting dirty.

3 Use a chamois leather or clean cloth to polish the irons, working up a good shine.

4 Put the irons together and thread them on to the leathers. Hook them on the stirrup bar.

Putting the bridle back together

1 Once you've cleaned and soaped the bridle, wash the bit but don't polish the mouthpiece.

2 Hold the headpiece with the throat-lash length on your left. Thread the browband through.

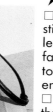

3 Buckle the bottom halves of the cheekpieces to their tops (attached to the headpiece).

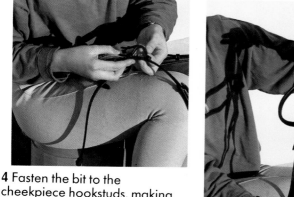

4 Fasten the bit to the cheekpiece hookstuds, making sure it's not upside down.

► If your pony's bit is a jointed snaffle, check that the flat sides are together.

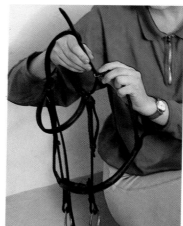

5 Thread the noseband through the headpiece and do it up. Attach the reins to the bit.

★ STIRRUP LEATHERS

☐ To re-assemble the stirrups, hold the leather with the buckle facing downward and toward you, pointed end away.

☐ Thread the point through the eye on top of the stirrup iron.

☐ Bring the leather up and back toward you, and fasten the buckle.

☐ Change over stirrup leathers so they take even stress. Otherwise the left one – which you mount by – stretches.

🐴 HOOKSTUDS AND BUCKLES

Hookstuds fold *in* toward the pony for neatness. Buckles face *outward* for comfort. Tuck strap ends inside their keepers and runners (the fixed and free loops on the straps).

And remember the noseband goes *inside* the cheekpieces.

Choosing foodstuffs

★ **CEREAL TYPES**

Most cereals (such as oats, bran and maize) are treated before being fed to horses and ponies, to open or remove the husks (outer layer). Whole cereals are harder to digest.

Clipped: The grains are cracked open, allowing the inner part of the grain to be digested easily.

Rolled: The cereals are put through a roller and broken apart slightly.

Flaked: The grains are flattened and cooked.

Cut: The husk is cut.

Extruded: The cereals are put through a 'mincing' machine to break them down.

Cracked: The cereals are lightly rolled to crack the husks.

Crushed: The cereals are broken up completely.

Micronized: The process involves pre-cooking cereals in a similar method to microwaving (from the inside, out), except that micronizing uses rays of infra-red light. This makes the energy-giving starch inside the cereal more digestible.

For information on general feeding tips see pages 106–109.

The range of foodstuffs available can make your choice difficult. Knowing a little about what's on offer helps you make the right selection.

Which food?

A pony's food requirements depend on his age, temperament, type, the amount of work he does, whether he lives in or out, his health, likes and dislikes. As a general rule grass-fed ponies need less concentrated food than stabled horses.

Grass nuts (or meal) consist of dried grass. They vary in protein content. Choose the lowest protein form you can, as a high content is only necessary for pregnant mares and young foals. You can add grass nuts to a pony's concentrate ration, or use it to supplement poor hay or grazing.

If your pony is allergic to dust, grass nuts make an ideal alternative to hay. Mix them with chaff (chopped up straw or hay), or chaff with molasses, to dilute them. Grass nuts are also good for balancing vitamin and mineral intake when fed with cereals, such as oats.

Wheatfeed meal is a cereal by-product of flour milling and needs careful balancing with minerals. It is best left in the hands of experts.

Locust bean meal is a product of the carob bean or locust bean tree. It is sweet and often included in compounds.

Oats are fed whole, clipped, rolled, flaked, cut, micronized or extruded. They are a useful energy source but many ponies 'hot up' on them. Oats need to be balanced with non-cereals such as dried grass or sugar beet.

Soya bean meal is high in protein. It is unnecessary for ponies over two years, except for elderly ponies with digestive problems.

Maize (corn) is a cereal. Many compound feeds contain flaked or micronized maize. It is rich in energy but low in fibre (unless on the cob) and should be fed with chaff (chopped hay), grass meal or sugar beet. As with all new foodstuffs, introduce it gradually into the diet.

Sunflower seed is a protein and energy source used in compounds.

Oatfeed meal is a cereal by-product used mainly in horse and pony nuts.

Barley is fed rolled, flaked, cut, micronized, extruded or boiled, but *not* whole. It contains more digestible energy than oats – because it has less husk and less fibre – making it a good mix with non-cereals.

Linseed cake is poor quality protein but is used to make coarse mixes more tasty. The oil helps coat condition.

grass nuts

wheatfeed meal

locust bean meal

whole oats

soya bean meal

whole maize

sunflower seeds

whole barley

oatfeed meal

linseed cake

Storing foodstuffs

★ OUTDOOR HAY AND STRAW

Hay and straw can be stored outside if necessary. Keep the bales raised off the ground on well-drained land and as sheltered as possible. Cover them with a large polythene sheet secured with a 'net' of binder twine. The cover can be weighted down by tying old tyres on to the net. On fine days remove the cover to let the hay 'breathe'.

▼ **Galvanized metal** feed bins are the most economical in the long term as they don't rust and are vermin proof. Plastic containers are easier to move around and are useful when going to a show.

Storing feed properly is essential to good hygiene. If you allow concentrated feed to become damp, it quickly rots – attracting mould and fungus. Your pony could become seriously ill if he eats feed in this condition. It's important, too, to make sure that your feed bins are protected against vermin, as rodents like rats can infect the feed itself with disease.

Careful storage of feedstuffs also saves money: hay exposed to rain can have some of the goodness washed from it and be quickly ruined.

Types of feedbins

The best sorts of storage bin for corn are made of galvanized metal. You can buy bins in all sizes and use them for any hard feed you wish. Those with two compartments mean you can fill each side in turn as you buy new feed.

Never buy more coarse mix or processed grain such as crushed barley or rolled oats than you can use within two weeks. Otherwise it could start to go bad. Cubes (nuts) and whole grain last for weeks or months if kept cool and dry. Molassed meal, sugar beet and chaff are best stored in a fridge in summer.

Always keep the bin lid down. Secure it with a small padlock to keep out ponies – and perhaps 'borrowers'!

Other materials such as sacks, plastic and fibreglass can all be chewed through by rats. Wood was used in the past and can be good if it's left natural and *not* treated with preservative which can taint the feed and cause poisoning.

Galvanized dustbins (refuse cans) are a safe compromise. You can tie down the lids even if you can't lock them.

All bins should be kept in cool, *dry* buildings – watch for leaky roofs dripping into them. Buildings made of metal or even wood heat up in summer unless well insulated.

Storing hay and straw

Hay and straw should be stored in *dry*, airy conditions. The building should be well ventilated – leave windows or top doors open. Old hay barns have ventilation bricks (bricks with drilled holes) installed.

It's best to stack bales off the ground, perhaps on wooden pallets. Leave enough space for a cat to squeeze underneath and root out rats and mice.

Don't store bales round the sides of indoor or outdoor riding arenas as they become covered in dust and unfit to feed. They should be stored downwind of the stables so any fungi and moulds present (even in good-quality fodder) blow away from the stables.

Plastic bins are a good temporary measure

Water containers

▼ Field troughs with a mains supply are best because your pony has a constant water supply.

Modern plumbing means that many fields have water supplies piped underground to troughs or taps. Piped water is a great advantage, as your pony has a permanent drinking supply and you don't have to carry large containers of water or use a hose pipe.

Troughs

Troughs are big enough to hold about as much water as a bath; automatic types have a reliable filling mechanism so they don't flood or dry up. Those with a plug hole make draining and cleaning easier.

There are two main sorts of filling mechanism. The first is the automatic ball-and-cock method. When the water is the correct height in the container the floating ball, which is attached to a metal arm, causes a cut-off device to stop water flowing. As the pony drinks, the level falls, the ball lowers and the water device opens allowing water in.

The other mechanism is a manually operated tap. You have to check the water level at least twice a day and turn on the tap to add water.

Whichever mechanism you have, it should be inside a strong cover at one end of the trough. This prevents the pony from injuring himself and stops him tampering with it.

Troughs are usually oblong, and made of galvanized metal, stone, heavy clay, plastic or glass-fibre. Plastic and glass-fibre troughs are safest because they cause less injury to ponies who collide with them. But these materials often crack if ponies chew them. Whichever type you choose there shouldn't be any sharp edges on which the pony could harm himself.

If you put the trough on a base to raise it off the ground, out of the mud, make sure the corners are rounded off to prevent leg injuries.

Drinking machines

Automatic drinking machines are quite common nowadays. Each stable has its own automatically filling container in the corner. It should be checked at least twice a day. Most 'auto-drinkers' hold about as much as a bucket.

Some are fitted with a meter so you can see how much the pony is drinking. The filling mechanism in each box is covered so that the horse or pony cannot fiddle with it.

Keep an eye on a pony who is not used to an auto-drinker. If he is reluctant to drink from it offer him water from a bucket until he becomes familiar with it.

To make sure the system is fitted properly it is best to get a plumber to do the job. If your stable is not fitted with an auto-drinker a water bucket, in a metal holder, is enough.

Salt and mineral licks

If your pony won't use a lick – perhaps because it makes his tongue sore – add a little salt to his feed every day instead. You should also do this for very hard-working ponies who may not be able to obtain enough salt from a lick.

Check with your vet or a nutritionist about how much to add – a dessertspoonful a day for a pony and a tablespoonful a day for a horse should be enough. Don't add it all to the same feed, and beware of adding too much at one time— it may put the pony off his feed.

If you are feeding prepared foods such as nuts or coarse mixes, check with your vet, as the salt content may already be adequate.

A salt lick should always be available in your pony's stable or field as salt is an essential part of his diet. It is particularly important in hot weather, especially during hard work, when the pony loses a lot of salt in his sweat.

Types of lick

A plain, iodized lick (containing iodine) should be the basic source of salt for any horse or pony. Commercially produced licks are oblong brick-shapes. You can also get natural rock salt, which is greyish in colour and comes in irregularly shaped chunks.

Licks are also available in a variety of flavours, such as mint, clove, cinnamon and aniseed. These are intended to get the pony to lick them more, so ensuring his salt supply.

You may have to try several flavours before you find one your pony likes. Always have a plain, iodized lick available anyway and treat specially flavoured ones as an extra.

You can also get 'mineralised' licks, which contain a range of other trace elements and minerals, as well as salt.

Salt lick holders

Special holders are available to take salt licks. They are either metal, plastic, or plastic-coated metal. Holders are simply the same shape as the lick with an open top and

▲ **Ponies at grass** should have a salt lick in the field or field shelter, or a special field feeding block which contains salt.

turned-up sides and bottom. You fix them to the stable wall at the pony's head height, and slide the lick in from the top.

Metal holders need checking regularly. Salt causes metal to rust, and rust from the holder may soak into the salt lick and contaminate it. Also, you need to replace the salt lick straight away when it is finished, because the metal holders have sharp edges.

If you get a plastic-coated holder check regularly that the coating is not chipping or cracking and, if it is, get another one.

Some horses like licks so much they actually bite chunks off them. In case this happens, don't site the holder over the water container. If a lump of salt falls into the water and dissolves, it taints the water and your pony won't drink it. This is very unpleasant for the pony, and it is bad for him to go without water.

Some people leave the lick in the horse's manger instead of in a holder. However, this can result in food being left congealed round the lick, which is unhygienic. The manger and the lick must be cleaned thoroughly after every feed.

► **Salt is a vital** part of the diet, and every horse should have a constant supply. Putting a salt or mineral lick in his stable is a convenient way of ensuring this.

metal holder

salt lick

mineral lick

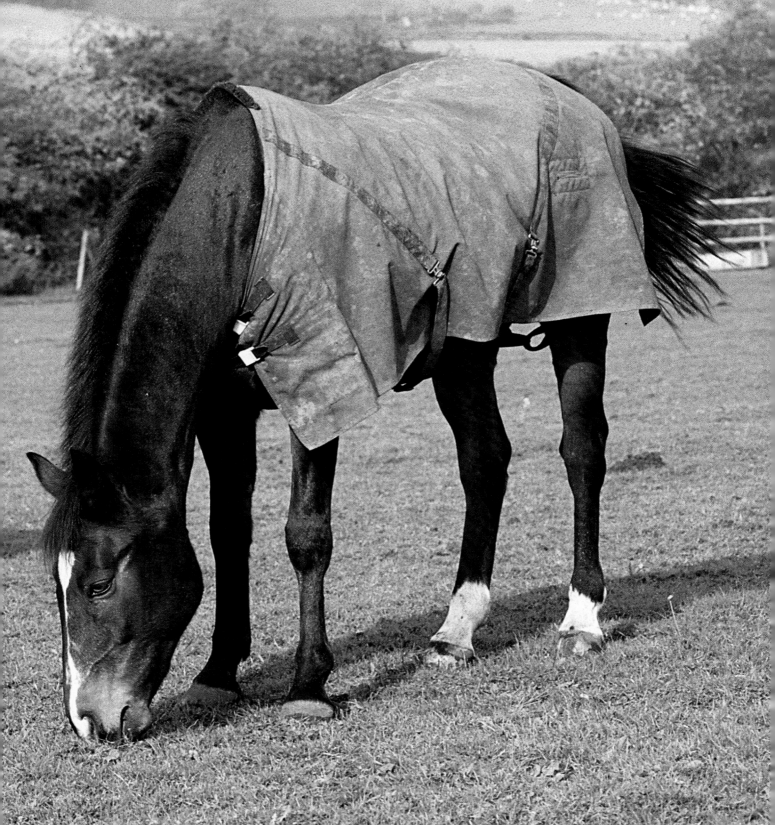

Maintaining a field or pasture

! THE WORM
• CYCLE

Ponies pick up and swallow worm larvae when grazing. The larvae travel through the body, causing damage and blockages, and end up as mature worms in the intestines, where they lay eggs.

These are passed out with the droppings on to the grass, hatch into larvae and the cycle begins again.

► **Droppings should** be removed from your pony's field at least once a week. This helps the grass to stay juicy and nutritious and keeps down the level of worms.

! GRASS
• CLIPPINGS

Many people imagine that grass clippings from a lawnmower are a treat for a pony.

This is only the case if they are *really* fresh. Clippings start to ferment within 15-20 minutes of the grass being cut. This fermentation process produces a build-up of gas in the pony's stomach which can be extremely harmful.

Whether they're from a garden next to your field, or on a grass verge beside a road, *don't* let your pony eat grass clippings.

Ponies enjoy living in a field because the outdoor life is natural to them. Make sure the pony in your care stays healthy and contented by frequently checking the field for hazards and looking after the grass.

Checking the field

Whenever you visit your pony, walk right round the field and check that everything is in good order.

Rubbish: Look over the ground carefully to make sure that there are no dangerous objects or litter lying around. Half-buried wire, rusty nails, glass or plastic bottles, empty crisp packets and sweet wrappers can all harm a pony.

Fencing: Look for weak spots or breaks in the fencing, so that you can get it repaired *before* the pony escapes. If the boundary is a hedge, check for gaps, particularly when the leaves have fallen in winter.

Shelter: Leafless trees and hedges also make less of a windbreak, and a field shed may be necessary for winter shelter. You need to watch out for changes *outside* the field as well — someone cutting down trees nearby can drastically alter the amount of wind through the field.

Wooden field shelters should be checked weekly for damage from kicks or general wear and tear. Loose, splintered boards weaken the structure and can cause injury.

Water: Every day, especially in summer, top up the water supply. Clean water troughs regularly and, if the trough is automatic, make sure it's refilling.

In winter, you can float a plastic football in the water. Its bobbing movement helps delay freezing. Use a neutral tone — a bright colour can frighten a timid pony. If ice still forms, break it morning and evening and remove it — otherwise the water will refreeze almost instantly. Pile the ice in a safe area *outside* the field to avoid accidents.

If a stream runs through the field, ask your vet how to have it checked for pollution. Do not use stagnant ponds as a water supply. The water is still, and more easily contaminated.

Removing droppings

Horses are fussy eaters — some grasses your pony will like and eat down to the soil; others he'll dislike and leave to grow long. Ponies also keep an area of the field for their droppings and they won't eat the grass there, either.

When a field becomes patchy with some bare areas and long, lank grass in other places, it is called 'horse-sick'. Try not to let your field get into this state. The first way of preventing it is to remove the bulk of your pony's droppings at least once a week. This encourages even grazing. You may be able to sell the droppings to keen gardeners.

Removing droppings also reduces the level of worms. Horse-sick paddocks not only have poor, sour grass but are riddled with worms. Worms in ponies can be the cause of poor condition, colic and, in extreme cases, death. Regular worming keeps the horse healthy and helps to reverse the cycle by reducing the level of worms in his droppings.

►**To keep tabs** on which field chores you've done each week, why not make your own checklist?
☐ Write or draw pictures of what needs checking across the top of a piece of card. List the days of the week down the side.
☐ Rule out a grid on a sheet of paper and tape it to the card so you have a daily box for each chore.
☐ At the end of the week, tear off the filled-in grid, ready to start again.

MY WEEKLY CHECKLIST	RUBBISH	HEDGE/FENCE	FIELD SHELTER	WATER	DROPPINGS	POISONOUS PLANTS
MONDAY						
TUESDAY	✓	✓		✓		
WEDNESDAY				✓	✓	
THURSDAY				✓		
FRIDAY	✓			✓		
SATURDAY	✓			✓		
SUNDAY	✓	✓		✓	✓	✓

Keeping your pony secure

Few moments can be more heart-breaking to a horse or pony owner than to have his or her much-loved animal stolen. Fortunately, there are several ways of deterring horse thieves. Whether your pony is stabled or at grass, the most effective is to have him freeze-marked.

What is freeze-marking?

Freeze-marking can be called 'cold branding'. Instead of a red-hot branding iron, super-chilled irons are used. This process is much more humane and pain-free than hot branding – but the results are just as permanent.

What happens during marking? First, the pony's coat is shaved around the marking area. The operator applies very cold irons to the coat and holds them on the skin for several seconds. This kills the pigmentation (colouring matter) in the skin. So when the hair regrows it is white, leaving a clearly visible code

number in the coat. Your pony is the only one with this number.

Grey ponies have the irons left on longer so the hair is killed completely, leaving the number in bare skin.

The mark is usually placed on the back, in the saddle area. When the pony is tacked up and ridden the number cannot be seen. But should the pony be found wandering loose or in a sale yard, the number can be spotted at once and checked. Some companies sell sew-on patches for rugs to warn thieves that the animal is marked.

Who freeze-marks?

There are several companies who freeze-mark, operating slightly different systems. The best keep a register of horses and their owners.

This means that the papers given to you at the time of marking prove you are the owner, and the number marked on to the pony can be checked against

▲ **Padlocks:** Make life difficult for a potential thief by securing the gate to the stable yard or field with a padlock and heavy chain. To stop the gate being lifted off, either reverse the top hinge or have a metal disc welded on to the hinge. Padlock *both* ends for good measure.

their register. If you sell the pony, the papers go with him and you inform the company of the change.

General security measures

As well as freeze-marking, you should take general precautions.

☐ Padlock the gate to the stable yard or field with a strong padlock and chain – at both ends if it can be lifted off its hinges.

☐ Ask local residents to tell you if strangers hang around the field. Give them your day and evening telephone numbers – and a 'thank-you' box of chocolates at Christmas!

☐ If you have a choice of field, opt for one with thick, prickly hedges around it. These are difficult for thieves to penetrate, while wooden and wire fencing can be taken down.

☐ Try not to leave a headcollar on your pony – it makes him easier to catch for other people as well as yourself.

Freeze-marking

This pain-free number marked on the back gives a horse permanent identification. If stolen, he can be easily traced. Avoid riding a pony for a few days after he's been marked, and use a numnah until the white hair has grown through. Freeze-marking makes no difference to a judge's decision when showing in-hand.

▼ **Having your pony stolen** leaves a hole in your life that nothing else can fill. So put off horse rustlers by getting your pony freeze-marked (cold branded).

You could also have a trip wire rigged up round the pony's field or stable. This is operated by battery, and sets off lights or an alarm if anyone intrudes.

Summer field care

▼ The pony's basic needs are the same summer and winter and you must check the field daily even when the weather is fine. The essentials are:

▲ Clean fresh water at all times

▲The right amount of quality food

▲ Overhead shelter from the sun

Long daylight hours make summer the most pleasant time for you to look after a grass-kept pony. But the pony himself can face problems – the main troubles created by sun, flies, hard ground and too much grass.

Rich pastures

Grass in summer can range from very rich to parched, dry and virtually useless. Surprisingly, the first kind is the most dangerous to ponies and cobs. These types are normally 'good doers', in other words, they do not need a lot of rich food and can become ill if they have access to it. They are better kept on poorish quality grazing – but they still have to have *something* to eat!

If the grass is lush and your pony looks quite fat enough – or even just well covered – you are safest to restrict his grazing. If you don't have a stable, try to move the pony on to poorer grazing, or strip-graze his field by dividing it up with electric fencing or use a muzzle for part of the day.

For ponies and cobs the type of grazing used for sheep is quite good enough. That used for cows, particularly dairy cattle, is usually far too rich.

Parched grazing

On the other hand, if the grass in your field is very short and sparse or shrivelled up because of prolonged dry weather, the pony may not be getting enough food and roughage. This can cause health problems of its own – like colic – apart from gradual weight loss.

If so, feed the pony hay, or a hay substitute such as one of the branded hayage products. Concentrates are not appropriate in this case.

If you are uncertain about how much hay to feed, give the pony the amount he would require if stabled, morning and night. Alternatively, check with your instructor or vet.

Feeding a field-kept pony in summer can be a fine balancing act. If you put him on an almost 'starvation diet' because you are frightened of him getting laminitis, you could find he gets so hungry he starts experimenting with poisonous plants and chewing the fences. If you feed him too much, he could contract laminitis after all. Always be ready to seek expert advice to get the balance right.

Water

Water sources must be checked at least twice daily in summer, particularly if they are not the self-filling type. In hot weather ponies can soon empty a large bin, or a trough if the filling mechanism has gone wrong.

Fresh clean water is vital to your pony's health and a careful eye must be kept on his supply.

Exercising the pony

If the pony is out all day, you do not *have* to exercise him yourself. But if you want him fit rather than just healthy, he needs ridden work and maybe a small feed of nuts. These give him extra energy and keep his muscles toned up for work as opposed to ambling about the field. His back muscles also need to be kept used to carrying your weight. ➤

★ **FIELD-SHARING**
If your pony is the only one receiving supplementary feeding in a field of several animals, you may have problems. Bring your pony out of the field at feeding times so that he gets his rations in peace without others stealing them. Then return him to the field when he has finished.

▼ **Summer sun** can reduce pasture to a mixture of scrub, thistles and dust with patches of grasses. In this case you should feed the pony hay morning and night.

Summer problems

The heat of summer brings out flies and other insects, and they cause some of the pony's worst problems.

Sweet itch: You can tell if your pony has sweet itch — caused by midges — because he will rub himself along the mane, shoulders, withers and tail. The condition can result in raw, infected skin which attracts flies even more, so do not think it will get better on its own. Call your vet as treatments are improving all the time.

The best preventive treatment is to stable the pony for two hours before and after dawn and sunset, when the midges are most active. If this is not possible, apply a fly repellant frequently.

Warble flies are much less common now than they used to be, but occasionally they crop up. If your pony develops hard, hot painful swellings in the saddle area, he could well have a warble maggot maturing in there. This is another task for your vet. He may need to get the maggot out and the pony will be off work until the wound heals — never ride a pony with such lumps on his back. Apart from the pain, you could kill the maggot which then rots under the pony's skin, setting up serious infection.

Bots: Pale-coloured eggs on your pony's legs and shoulders are bot eggs. If the pony licks them and swallows them he will have bots in his stomach all winter, unless you worm him in autumn with a medicine effective against them. You should give him a general wormer anyway, but if you see the eggs, scrape them off gently with a blunt knife or plastic spatula. Again a good fly repellant prevents the flies from landing to lay the eggs in the first place.

▼ **A rubbed tail** is often a sign of sweet itch, an irritating skin allergy caused by midges. Ask your vet for a lotion to alleviate the itching.

► **Fly fringes,** when used as well as a repellant, bring great relief to a pony.

▼ **Rich grazing** is hazardous as ponies can get the disease laminitis if they gorge themselves.

To keep a field-kept pony fit for weekend work such as shows, aim to ride him for about an hour or more on three weekdays. A lesson once a week reminds you about good riding techniques and keeps your pony working correctly and using the right muscles.

Shelter and shade

Do see that your pony has *proper* shelter and shade *overhead*. This means trees, high, overhanging hedges or a field shed to help him get away from too much sun.

However, the most effective way to protect him against flies is to apply a really good fly repellant (the type known as 'residual' is best because its effects last several days). This stops the flies landing on him to start with.

The daily check

Your daily check should include the pony, the ground, the water and the fencing.

The pony should show all the usual signs of good health – he should be alert, with a shiny coat. If he seems unusually quiet, dozy, perhaps unco-ordinated and standing on his own, he could be ill. In hot weather it is possible for animals with no proper shelter to get heatstroke. Check him for wounds and his feet for chipping horn if the ground is hard, and loose or missing shoes. Flies can cause ponies to gallop in desperation, jarring legs and feet.

Check the field for litter thrown in by passers-by, if they have access to the field, and remove everything you find. Take rubbish well away from the field and dispose of it properly — don't just dump it somewhere.

Check the water supply, which must be plentiful and clean, and finally check the fencing. Hedges, too, need to be looked at as leaves disguise gaps which the pony knows are there. You may need to fix rails across to close them up. Make sure the shelter is sound and remove droppings, which otherwise attract flies.

! VANDALISM
If you suspect your pony has been subject to vandalism – perhaps he has unexplained wounds, seems upset or tired, has had his mane or tail cut or your gate or field has been tampered with – tell the police at once.

▼ **Hosing down** after a sweaty ride is appreciated on a hot day! But don't let the horse become chilled afterwards.

Winter field care

Although many ponies are hardy, none can be left to fend for themselves in a field. In the wild, ponies roam over large areas of land and can shelter in woods and valleys or on hillsides. A domesticated pony is a 'prisoner' in a field which, left to itself, may offer no real shelter, little natural food, and may become badly poached.

Keeping a pony warm

The best way to keep your pony warm is to leave on his full winter coat, mane and tail, and provide plenty of shelter, overhead as well as side on. An unclipped, native-bred pony should not need a New Zealand rug but a finer-bred one or clipped pony does, and must have a proper field shed.

A New Zealand rug is waterproof, made from synthetic (probably nylon) fabric or canvas. It should be shaped to fit the pony, curving to fit his backbone, and darted at elbow and hip. Good makes have no surcingle, but fasten at the breast and with hindleg straps.

Put the rug on like a stable rug; fasten the leg straps then the breast straps. To remove, unfasten the breast strap and

▼ **A clipped pony** should be turned out in a New Zealand rug in winter. A neck and hood attachment keeps him extra warm.

then the leg straps, and slide it off.

Take the rug off twice daily and check the pony for signs of chafing (rubbed hair or bald patches) or sore places, particularly at the withers, shoulders, hips and between the hindlegs. You really need two rugs so you can keep them fairly clean and dry in turn.

Grooming

Every day, pick out the feet and check the condition of legs, shoes and feet. Damp-sponge discharges and dirt from eyes, nostrils, sheath and dock and dry these areas with an old towel. Brush out the mane and tail to stop them becoming too tangled.

Do not body brush an outdoor pony. Unless you're riding, you don't even have to brush off mud every day as it protects against the wind. If the mud is wet, it won't brush off anyway, so if you want to ride, you have to dry the mud by thatching (covering the back in straw under a rug), then brush it off.

Feeding

The most important food is good hay because winter grass contains almost no nourishment. Buy hay from hay and

▼ Breaking the ice: In really cold weather, the water supply may freeze. You must break the ice and remove it from the trough to slow down re-freezing. Take it outside the field where the pony won't slip on it.

Check the water supply daily

► Filling a hay net:
Loosen the drawstring and open the neck. Shake the hay thoroughly to get rid of any dust, and pack it down into the net.

straw merchants or animal feed firms; your instructor can recommend a reputable firm.

Stress that you want *good* hay. Meadow or mixture hay is ideal for ponies and it contains varied grasses. Good hay should smell sweet, not musty.

There must be *no* mould (white, green or black powdery patches) or dust when you shake it out. Bad hay is dangerous to your pony's health. He may even

! IS YOUR PONY COLD?

A cold pony looks miserable, maybe hunched up, with his tail to whatever shelter there is. He may shiver, and his coat may stand up when it's dry.

Feel the lower half of his ears: if they are cold the pony's body is cold all over. He may even feel too unhappy to move about and warm himself up.

Don't let him stay like this or he could get hypothermia (a serious chill). Bring him into a stable or shed, dry him, put on a rug and stable bandages and give him hay and a feed.

Use a New Zealand rug on him in cold, wet, windy weather and have a field shelter erected.

Tying a hay net

1 Lift the full hay net up to the height of the ring. Pull the drawstring tight and pass it through the ring. Loop the string through a square mesh low down in the net.

2 Pull it taut and hoist the net up tightly so that it doesn't lower too much as it empties. Pass the rope end round the back of the drawstring and pull a loop through. Tighten it. You now have a quick-release knot.

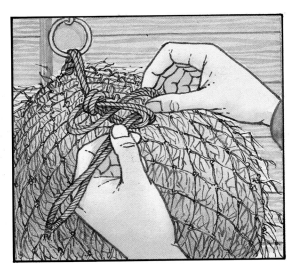

3 To stop the pony tugging the end and undoing the knot, make another loop with the end of the drawstring. Check that the net is high enough to stop the pony catching his feet in the mesh even when it empties. The knot may tighten as the pony eats from the net, but you can easily undo it by pulling the end.

MISTAKE!

Don't tie the hay net up loosely so that it sags down. The net must also be attached to a firm support so the pony has something to push against when he takes out the hay, and is best kept under shelter from the rain.

refuse to eat it although very hungry.

Ponies should have *ad lib* hay (as much as they will eat) in winter. Your pony needs about a third of a bale a day.

Feeding hay loose on the ground is wasteful, and cattle-type field hay-racks are dangerous for ponies. Use a hay net.

To fill a hay net, open up the neck, shake out the hay thoroughly and cram it down into the net. When full, pull the drawstring tight. Hang it at the pony's head height against the wall of the shelter (inside) or against a tree trunk, as he has to push it against something firm to get the hay out. You can also fasten a net to the top rail of wooden fencing, but it's better to keep the hay away from rain.

Extreme weather
You need to take extra special care of your pony when it's very cold or wet.
● In frost, break the ice on water supplies twice daily. Floating a plastic football in the trough helps delay freezing. Take all the ice out of the water otherwise it quickly re-freezes.
● If waterlogged areas of the field start to freeze over, cover them with a thick layer of used bedding, sand or grit,

otherwise the pony could slip and fall over.
● You may need to give extra food during extreme weather, to help keep the pony warm and because what grass there is may be buried under snow.
● Check the hard ground is not breaking the hooves of unshod feet; if it is, call the farrier to put on light shoes. Prevent snow from balling in the hooves by smearing the soles with old cooking fat or oil (not axle grease or engine oil which can damage horn and skin).
● The pony's face can get chapped if his eyes water, especially in windy weather. Bathe with clear water containing a little antiseptic and apply a water-resistant antiseptic cream.
● It's safest to bring ponies into a stable or barn during storms or very severe weather.
● During heavy rain, ponies can become soaked to the skin and very cold. They must have proper overhead shelter; a steady downpour comes through trees, however dense. The ground becomes very muddy, particularly round gateways, troughs and shelter entrances. Spread thick layers of straw or used bedding here and top up regularly.

! LOSING WEIGHT
● A thick coat can hide a thin pony. Push your fingers right through the coat. If you can feel his ribs, increase his hay allowance, worm him and have his teeth checked by the vet.

▼ When it snows, make sure the pony has extra hay to eat as he can't easily get at what grass there is. He needs enough food to keep up his body heat as well as to give him energy.

Catching a pony

Most ponies are easy to catch but some play hard to get. Fortunately, it's a bad habit that can usually be changed with patience and persistence. And it's worth the effort because grass-kept ponies should be caught and checked over every day.

When all goes well

The right way to catch a well-behaved pony is to walk up quietly where he can see you. Hold a headcollar or halter in one hand and a titbit in the other (some really willing ponies don't even need a titbit). Don't approach from behind: if a pony can't see you and you startle him, you could get kicked.

Slide your leadrope over his neck behind his ears as you give him a titbit. Hold the rope together under his throat as you put on the headcollar or halter. You might feel as if you need three hands to begin with, but you'll soon get used to managing.

Attracting his attention

Handling a pony is much easier if he answers to his name – but most don't! Use his name whenever you approach him, before a command, to attract his

attention or to keep his concentration. Fuss him when he responds until it becomes second nature. Then when you enter his field and call, he'll probably come at once, especially if you have a titbit that he likes.

It helps if the titbit is something the pony can't resist. A pony who's just filled himself with grass won't find fresh food like carrot or apple appealing because it's too similar. Take something completely different – dried food like coarse mix or pony nuts, for example.

For those who really need tempting, such everyday feed may not be attrac-tive enough. Find out what your pony has a weakness for and take that. Most have a sweet tooth and love sugar lumps or hard mints.

Turning him out

When you turn your pony out into the field, be calm and gentle. Don't surprise him, slap him on the bottom, shout and whoop or be rough. If the pony associ-ates catching and turning out with excitement, rush and hassle, he'll expect this and become difficult. Remember the perfect combination – quiet, firm con-fidence and irresistible titbits!

▼ **Hard to get:** Many ponies know being caught means work and, understandably, they walk away as soon as you approach.

The trick is to turn catching into a treat – sometimes just make a fuss of the pony and let him go again. And remember the most vital ingredient – his favourite titbit!

When things go wrong

There are several ways to make catching a mischievous pony easier.

First, leave a headcollar on with a 15cm (6in) length of binder twine knotted to the bottom ring. This gives you something to take hold of. Offer the pony his favourite titbit with two hands and slip one under his chin to hold the twine. Do not use rope because it is dangerous – the twine must break if the pony puts his foot on it.

Many ponies don't really like work and know what's in store for them when they're caught. Break this pattern by catching the pony *without* working him. Give him a titbit, put his headcollar on and look him over for injury. Then let him go. Every now and then, go to the field just to inspect the fencing, water supply and so on, without going near him. He'll come to regard you as part of the scenery.

You can extend this idea by walking 'aimlessly' about the field, close to and away from him. Walk casually past him and catch the binder twine on his headcollar. Give him his titbit and leave it at that. He'll never know what to expect with this routine. The technique requires considerable patience, as running after the pony if he canters off undoes all your good work.

Sometimes, having a squeaky toy

Catching a willing pony

1 Approach the pony quietly from the front where he can see you. Hold the headcollar behind your back.

2 Offer him the titbit from the flat of your hand. A grass-fed pony is tempted by pony nuts or sugar lumps.

3 Slip the leadrope round his neck behind the ears. Use one hand to secure it under his throat.

4 Once you've put the noseband on, pull the main strap round behind his ears and buckle it up.

Finally, thank him with a pat.

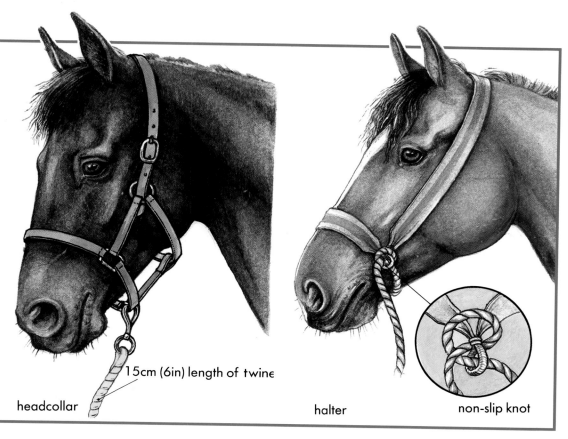

Headgear

A headcollar that's made of leather looks like a heavy bridle with no bit or browband. But nowadays many are made of nylon webbing and come in bright colours. The leadrope clips to the ring under the jaw.

With a tricky pony, leave the headcollar on with a 15cm (6in) length of twine attached, giving you something to hold.
A halter (made of rope or webbing) is combined with its leadrope. Always use the special knot to stop the rope tightening.

15cm (6in) length of twine

headcollar

halter

non-slip knot

helps – most ponies can't resist coming up to investigate the noise! Also, a large, rustly bag full of food that *you* are eating often works. Just stand still in the field and, when the pony comes for his share, wander towards the gate without giving him any – until he lets you catch him.

Drastic measures

If catching your pony turns into a real problem, you'll have to take more drastic action.

Herding a pony into a corner with several people holding a long rope occasionally works, as long as it is done quietly and craftily. The rope should be about 1m (3ft) off the ground, and kept in a straight line until he's cornered and caught. However, some ponies get wise to this trick and learn to charge, bite and kick, so only herd as a last resort.

One of a herd

With a pony that is a problem to catch you'll find it much easier to keep him on his own in a field. Having a companion is likely to excite him all the more, and there's nothing more exasperating than seeing two friends galloping gleefully to the other end of the field!

Other horses also get in the way, try to eat the titbits meant for your pony and may chase him if he is timid.

When you have no choice but to keep your pony with others, you may have to act bossily to make the unwanted ones stay away. However, loud, frantic behaviour may excite the herd into charging about, making your task totally impossible.

A sharp slap on the breast (never the head except for biting) with a firm growl – 'No!' – keeps most pushy ponies back. Behave calmly and confidently and, if the field contains a real bully, take a friend to help you cope.

Be particularly careful that other horses don't escape when you are leaving the field with your pony. A catching pen at the entrance (as in the picture below), with a second gate shutting off the escape route, helps to separate one pony from the rest.

Catching pen

A pen at the field entrance helps when you're singling out one pony from several. Instead of one gate, there are two which enclose a small space. Even if a pony escapes through the first gate his exit is blocked by the second.

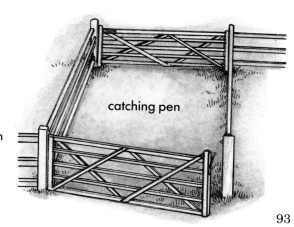

catching pen

Exercise plans for a . . .

▼ **Even when out hacking,** you can school your horse. Make sure he is concentrating and attentive to what you ask him to do. Practise smooth transitions and aim for rhythmical strides in all paces.

The fat, round sleekness of a pony at grass indicates perfect health but not physical fitness for work. Although you can never get a field-kept pony to the hard condition needed for regular hunting or competition work, you can make him fit enough for local shows and events, occasional hunting or limited endurance riding. Before you ask him to work, the pony needs a programme of exercise routines to build up his strength gradually.

...*grass-kept pony*

What is fitness?

Horses in the wild are nomadic, roaming widely over large areas where they gain natural exercise and variety of diet. In the confines of a field, a pony depends on you to recognize and correct any deficiencies that occur.

Exercising the pony means he can perform to the best of his ability without stress and strain. It strengthens his limbs and tendons, lowering the risk of sprains during exertion. It conditions and tones his muscles and reduces the amount of fat he carries. By decreasing the size of his belly, there's more room for his lungs – this eases the pony's breathing and lets him work more efficiently.

Feeding for fitness

It is unnatural for a horse to work and a diet of grass doesn't give him enough energy. Fitness is achieved by a combination of diet and exercise. The intake of energy foods must equal or slightly exceed the output of energy. A very rough guide is 450g of concentrated food for each 1.5km, or 1lb to each mile of ground covered. But you must also take into account the size of the pony and his character (high-spirited ponies need less concentrates).

The supply of concentrates, preferably balanced pony nuts, should be further increased for several days before a demanding occasion. Divide feeds into two a day and give them at the same times so that you establish a regular

The value of a pony's grass intake varies enormously according to the condition of his pasturage.
● **Early spring** may mean that you should restrict the area available to the pony so the grass can grow. Increase his hay ration accordingly.
● **Mid-summer:** On lush pasture, smaller ponies can become too fat. They should be switched to more sparse paddocks where they have to move around to get their food.

pattern. Allow at least 1-1½ hours for digestion before you saddle up the pony for exercise.

A pony – being much hardier than a horse – generally does better at grass and is more manageable. Keep a close watch on his appearance and behaviour. If the pony is excessively skittish too many oats are the likely cause. If he's lazy and sluggish, increase the energy foods. Fatness means the pony is eating too much and a poor and ribby appearance means you should increase the rations – but worm the pony regularly in case this is the cause of poor condition.

Recognizing his condition

In a 'soft' condition the pony's muscles are slack, he is fat with a gross belly and he cannot make a sustained effort without sweating and distress.

In a 'poor' condition the pony appears thin, has a 'staring' coat, is weak with a depressed expression and lacks energy.

The hard condition brought about by correct diet and exercise means he is free of extra fat and his muscles and tendons are toned up so that he can perform at the peak of his ability.

Changing the diet

A pony should always have the same daily weight of food, but the content of this depends on the work required of him. As you work him harder, so he needs more energy foods.

You must carry out all changes to the diet gradually. A 14-14.2-hand pony, weighing about 400kg (900lbs), needs about 9-10kg (20-22lbs) daily. For an unfit, grass-kept pony, this can consist entirely of bulk food: grass or grass and hay. A pony in full daily work needs two

---

The six-week exercise programme

At every stage of the programme, aim to encourage the pony into a free, forward movement with an even rhythm at all speeds. A good average is 9.5km/h (6mph). An irregular, jerky gait, and quick changes of pace over short intervals

make the pony lose concentration. The feeding amounts suggested are for a 14.2-hand pony weighing about 400kg (900lbs). If your pony is smaller, reduce the weight of the feed, but keep the proportions the same.

Week 1-2: Begin with walking only, initially for an hour, every day if possible and at least three times a week if not. Increase gradually up to 2½ hours' steady walking over sloping ground along varied routes.
Feeding: Morning and evening feeds — ½kg (1lb) of pony nuts or other concentrates to supplement his daily intake of 9kg (19lbs) of grass and hay according to season.

Week 2-3: After ten 'walking only' sessions, introduce increasing lengths of trotting into the rides. Always start out and finish with a ten-minute walk. This loosens up the pony at the beginning and cools him on return. Ride him on a long rein on the way back to relax him. Trotting up and down hills reduces the amount of fat a pony carries as well as conditioning and toning his muscles.
Feeding: Gradually increase the two feeds in quantity to ¾kg (1½lbs) each.

thirds bulk and one third concentrated food with an increased proportion of concentrates before a demanding event.

Which concentrates?

The concentrated part of the feed can consist of a variety of foodstuffs. The most suitable are balanced pony nuts. Check on the variety and content, and follow the manufacturer's instructions: these contain some bulk so you can reduce the hay ration. The bulk content also means the pony eats the feed slowly. However, pony nuts are the most expensive way of feeding your pony.

Other concentrates you can use are oats, which are best bruised and fed with bran; barley, which should be fed flaked or boiled and is less 'heating' than oats; flaked maize; cooked linseed fed as a mash; and sugar beet pulp which should be mixed with cereals or nuts as

it is unsuitable as a staple food on its own. You can add cut-up apples or carrots to feeds, give split peas and beans in small quantities and feed swedes and turnips whole.

Divide the daily ration of concentrates into two regular feeds, and three as the ration increases. Divide the daily hay ration into two and give it in a hay net morning and evening. The second ration should be the larger so the pony can munch through the night.

Preparing the pony

You may want your pony fit for sharp bursts of energy as in show jumping, for prolonged effort as in eventing or hunting or for slow, steady exertion like pulling a trap. Whatever your aims, there are several points to bear in mind when planning your fitness programme.
□ Allow at least six weeks of prep-

● **Late summer:** Very dry conditions may mean the pasture becomes bare. Supplement the hay and keep a careful eye on the water supply.
● **Mid-winter** delay in supplementing the grass can cause loss of condition. The pony needs extra rations to keep warm, particularly if he is thin. It is now that the 'warming' foods like barley, maize (corn), split peas and beans, and turnips can be added to the diet.

Week 4: On suitably soft but not deep ground — never road surfaces, stony tracks or heavy mud — you can start gentle cantering during the fourth week of daily exercise. Make sure he has the correct bend on turns and a good, balanced carriage. He should be alert and responsive to your aids.
Feeding: Introduce a midday feed of ½kg (1lb) of concentrates.

Week 5-6: Start short gallops during the fifth or sixth week depending on the pony's condition.
Feeding: Gradually increase the size of each feed so that the pony has 3kg (6½lbs) of concentrated food per day — one third of his daily rations in high energy foods. This should be increased to half the ration (5kg/11lbs) for two days before a demanding event. If your pony is lazy, you could change very slowly from pony nuts to oats for energy build-up and go back to nuts or other less heating foods after the occasion.

aration before asking a pony in soft condition to make strenuous efforts.

☐ The unfit pony must be shod before he can begin work on roads or hard ground.

☐ The build-up should be a *gradual* progression – this is the aim in planning your exercise routine.

☐ Girth galls and saddle sores are especially likely on soft, fat ponies. Make sure the pony is dry and mud-free in the saddle area before tacking up. Don't push the pony too fast or you may damage his legs, in which case you have to throw the whole programme out and rest him until he's recovered.

Varying the routine

To keep both your own and the pony's interest, vary the daily exercises within the general pattern of gradual development. Try to find several routes which offer long sections of firm grass track and ride over them in alternating direc-

▲ **As the pony gets fitter**, you can jump practice fences after schooling your pony or going out for a hack.

► **Schooling sessions** should be kept brief and if possible be followed by a ride out to stop the pony becoming bored.

If he has a very thick coat and sweats excessively when ridden, it is worth trace-clipping the pony and protecting him with a New Zealand rug in the winter months. Heavy sweating causes loss of condition.

tions. This avoids boredom and habits like 'we always gallop here' starting with a buck or two to show that he knows!

In the later stages of the exercise schedule, try spending the first half hour schooling your pony in the paddock. Practise bending and turning and keeping his attention on your aids.

If you can, put up several small but sturdy jumps at the side of the paddock. Pop the pony over these for practice after a schooling session or after a short ride when his fitness has improved. Take advantage of any suitable, natural obstacles to jump when you are out on rides. Always check the landing as well as the take-off side before attempting a jump.

Exercises in the school or over jumps should continue for 20 to 30 minutes – no longer. Always finish with a happy note of achievement, never after an unsuccessful tussle.

Carry out the daily rides and exercises sometimes alone and sometimes with others. Calm companions can be particularly useful for solving problems like traffic shyness or refusing to leave home. And going with friends adds to the fun and variety of the routines.

Keeping a pony fit

Daily exercise to maintain fitness is ideal to keep a pony prepared for special occasions but not essential otherwise. A minimum of three, two-hour sessions spaced through the week will keep up the pony's condition.

After a demanding day out – at a show or hunting – let the pony rest in his field for 24 hours. Just check him over for damage and lead him about for ten minutes to relieve stiffness and make sure he's sound. The next day you can go back to his normal routine.

CHOOSING YOUR TIME
Try to carry out your fitness programme during a long holiday period. This means that you can ride your pony daily, or almost every day. It also means you can give him a third feed at midday as the schedule progresses.

▼ **Place the feed** in a portable manger firmly hooked on to the top of the gate or fence where the pony may eat his rations undisturbed.

4 Stabled ponies

Bedding

▲ **Tie up your pony** in a safe place away from the stable when mucking out.

★ **TYPES OF BEDDING**
Many materials make good bedding for horses, so be guided by what you can find easily in your area.

NON-ABSORBENT bedding needs to be mucked out every day. The most common is **straw**; wheat straw is best. **Bark** is also suitable, but takes several years to rot down into useful manure.

ABSORBENT materials need a full mucking out less often. They include:
Peat: Difficult to spot the dung! Good for horses with dust allergies and makes the best manure.
Fallen pine needles: Use the long, soft type.
Paper: Usually shredded. Avoid very long pieces which wrap round the legs.
Sawdust is good as long as it's not dusty.

◄ **Wood shavings** are a good choice. They are coarser than sawdust and therefore more dust free. Make sure they are safe for animals (not sprayed).

Bedding is important for two reasons: it provides a soft cushion for a pony to lie on and makes it easier to keep the stable clean.

How bedding helps

Horses are heavy and don't like lying on hard surfaces. If they do they may hurt their legs, and to avoid this, are more likely to remain standing up. This in turn causes stress. So make sure you give your pony a soft layer of bedding.

As well as warmth and comfort, bedding is important for hygiene. Stale, wet bedding can easily be removed and replaced with a fresh layer. Droppings are kept off the ground: where there is no bed the floor becomes slippery.

What to use

A wide range of materials makes suitable bedding. It should be dry, clean, easy to manage and not harmful to the pony. Sometimes horses are allergic to dust and react badly to fine materials like sawdust.

Some materials let urine pass right through and are called non-absorbent or draining. Other beds soak up wetness and are called absorbent or non-draining.

The list on the left gives you an idea of what products you can use. These vary from one area to another. If you live near a saw mill use wood shavings or sawdust; in other places peat or straw may be easily available.

Night and day beds

If your pony is stabled overnight, he needs a 'full' bed. The whole floor should be thickly covered with banks at the sides, because bare floors lose heat and chill the stable. A full bed is comfortable, shuts out draughts and keeps the horse warm. Pack it down well so the horse can walk about easily.

Leave gaps under the hay net, so the pony eats any spilled hay, and in front of the door, so the bed does not overflow into the yard when the door is opened.

For a pony that is only stabled during the day, a full bed is less important. A smaller 'day' bed does not need banks and occupies only half the floor – enough to lie on, but quick to tidy up!

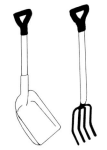

SHOVEL AND FORK
When buying a shovel, choose one with a deep pan so you can clear away large amounts in one go.

The number of prongs required on the fork varies with the type of bedding. The finer the bedding the more you need: four is enough for straw, but eight is better when working with, say, sawdust.

Equipment for cleaning a stable. A bucket or laundry basket is a good substitute for the old-fashioned 'skep' and is for putting droppings in. Use a rubber glove or a pair of boards about 30cm (1ft) long for removing droppings by hand.

You also need a stiff broom, a fork with curved prongs and a shovel with a large pan and curved sides. Use lightweight tools with long handles so you don't get back ache. The barrow should be light, but large enough to avoid repeated trips to the muck heap.

Other useful items are a garden sheet to cover the barrow and to carry spare bedding and a rake for levelling the bed.

Cleaning up

★ **WHEN TO BANK UP**
Normally you can leave gaps in the bedding under the hay net and by the door. But if your pony is ill, or you are looking after a mare that is about to foal, cover the floor completely and extend the banks to include the back of the door and keep out any draughts.

There are three different routines for cleaning a stable, all part of the process of 'mucking out'.

Skipping out is a quick tidy up. You only remove the droppings. The name comes from the skip (or skep) – the traditional basket for the droppings. Nowadays, a laundry basket or plastic bucket serves the purpose just as well.

Setting fair means making the pony comfortable for the night. The bed is tidied up, and a few other chores done, such as refilling the water bucket and picking out the hooves.

A full muck out includes going right down to the floor and doing a complete clean-up job.

Skip out a deep litter of absorbent bedding, such as peat, several times during the day. You don't need to do a full muck out more than once a week. But muck out non-absorbent beds such as straw fully each day. Always set the bed fair in the evening.

A full muck out

Before starting to muck out, remove the feed bowl, water bucket and hay net from the stable. Put the pony in another stable or paddock, or tie him up in a safe place. Collect together all your tools. Park the barrow in the doorway and prop up the other tools against the wall or door where they are safe and convenient.

Skip out first, removing all the drop-

► **How often** you muck out varies according to the type of bedding. In this stable, wood shavings are used. Because they are absorbent, the box is given a full muck out once a week.

Every day, the stable is skipped out and tidied up, and the sides banked up.

Mucking out a stable

1 Most horses push the bedding toward the door during the night, so use the broom to sweep it back from the entrance.

2 With a rubber glove or two short planks of wood, pick up the droppings and put them in the bucket.

5 Let the floor air and dry out if possible. Shake up the clean bedding and level it out with the fork.

6 Wheel the dirty bedding off to the manure heap straightaway – don't leave it lying about in the barrow.

pings, and empty them into the barrow.

Take the dung fork and either pile all the clean bedding from one half of the box to the other half, or pile it from the middle to the sides. Leave behind any droppings you missed earlier, and the wet and dirty bedding. Sweep all this into a pile at the front of the box and shovel it into the barrow.

If you are working from one side to the other, put all the bedding to the clean half of the box. Finish the second half in the same way as the first.

Swill out the drain (if there is one) with a bucket of water. Check that it is draining.

Leave the stable to air for a while, and let the floor dry.

Bedding down

Use the dung fork or a pitch fork and shake up the clean bedding. Spread it evenly over the floor, piling it more thickly at the sides. Use the back of the fork to compress the banks of bedding against the walls. Level the surface of the bedding in the middle of the box, and check the depth with the fork – the bed should come up to at least the depth of the prongs.

Top up if necessary with extra bedding, shaking it well before you level everything off.

Refill and replace the water bucket and hay net. Try to allow about half an hour for any dust to settle before you return the pony to his clean box.

SAFE AND SOUND

Always follow these rules when mucking out:

☐ DO keep the tools hanging up safely, prongs facing the wall, when not in use.

☐ DO wear a mask if the bedding is dusty. Better still – avoid using dusty bedding in the first place.

☐ DON'T muck out with the horse in the box. If there's nowhere else to put him, tie him up and keep the tools well away from his legs.

☐ DON'T neglect mucking out – your pony will be miserable and unhealthy.

3 Fork the clean bedding to the sides of the box, leaving behind the hard wet shavings underneath.

4 Shift the dirty bedding into the wheelbarrow, then brush any clean bedding to the sides, so the floor is clean.

7 Collect more bedding if necessary. Tip out the new on top of the old – enough for a bed the depth of the fork prongs.

8 Mix all the bedding thoroughly, banking up the sides and leaving gaps around the door and under the hay net.

Feeding a stabled pony

A pony in a stable relies totally on people to care for him. After fresh air and water, the correct food is his most important need.

Nature and the horse

In the wild, ponies spend most of their time grazing. Often the grass is very poor and they need to eat plenty of it to get enough nourishment.

Nature has designed the digestive system to allow for this. The horse has a small stomach, suitable for always containing a little, but never too much at any one time. So try to imitate this feeding pattern for a stable-kept pony.

The pony needs plenty of bulk food – usually hay. The 'short', energy-giving, concentrated feeds like oats should be small and fed twice or even three times

◄ **Feed your horse** little and often because this is how he eats in the wild. Feeding from the floor is also natural, but can be wasteful if the bucket tips up.

a day so he eats little and often.

Aim to include something fresh each day, such as carrots or apples, because horses by nature eat fresh grass, not dry hay and short feeds.

When to feed

Feed your pony at regular intervals three or four times a day. Make sure he has water by him all the time. If you think he's thirsty, water him *before* you feed him. Drinking a lot after a feed can be harmful.

Avoid riding a pony for at least one hour after he has eaten to give the stomach time to empty. The horse may get colic if he is ridden immediately after feeding.

After riding, let the pony eat a little hay before a short feed. This takes the edge off his hunger and stops him gobbling the food too fast. Slow down a really greedy pony by putting a brick or some large stones in the manger so he has to work harder to find his meal.

▲ **Fresh food:** A stabled pony misses out on grass – his natural diet. Make up for this by giving him something succulent in his feed every day, such as apple.

sugar beet

oats

pony nuts

bran

◄ **Foodstuffs** suitable for a pony.
Oats are the traditional 'short' feed for horses. They are nutritious and easily digested but can over-excite ponies.

Sugar beet is sold dry. It gives the horse energy and is good roughage. Before feeding, soak it for 12–18 hours in about two and a half times as much water as beet.

Horse and pony nuts (cubes or pellets) contain concentrated ingredients, bulk feeds, vitamins and minerals. The exact mixture varies according to make.

Bran: Small amounts of bran can be used with oats. Alternatively, bran can be fed as a mash before a rest day or if the pony is ill.

WATER ON TAP

All ponies should have a constant supply of clean water. Refill the buckets with fresh water at least twice a day, even if the pony hasn't drunk it all.

Unless your stable is fitted with an 'auto-drinker' that refills automatically, two large buckets, or even a small dustbin of water, are ideal.

Remove the handles from buckets left in the stable, and secure them in a bucket holder or wedge them into a motor tyre for safety.

automatic drinker

⭐ SALT

This is the most important mineral for ponies. They need it every day because salt is lost in sweat and urine. Without salt, a pony may start chewing wood or eating his droppings.

Either provide a salt lick so the pony can help himself, or add one tablespoonful of salt to the evening feed.

► **Hay** should make up the bulk of your pony's diet. Fill up the hay net at least twice a day.

What to feed

Most ponies keep well on a diet almost entirely made up of hay. Make sure it is good quality – greenish, weed-free, succulent and sweet-smelling – and between 4–18 months old. If your pony is too fat, you can use clean feed straw rather than hay. Straw comes from cereals: choose oat or barley straw because wheat straw is not very tasty.

Short feeds of oats give most ponies too much energy, so usually just horse and pony nuts (cubes) are enough. Always give short feeds according to the work the pony is doing, his temperament and also his rider's ability. A fired-up pony is not a good idea for a novice rider.

How much to feed

The amount of food to give a horse depends on his size – the larger the pony, the more food he needs. In scientific terms, horses eat 2–2½% of their body weight a day. So a pony around 14 hands high, weighing about 300–400kg (660–880lbs), needs a total of 7½–10kg (16½–21lbs) food a day.

If the pony is healthy and not doing any work, all this food can be hay. As his exercise increases, so he needs some short feed. The hay should be reduced so he still gets the same *weight* of food – only the proportions change.

Give the hay in two lots and split the short feed. This gives four feeds a day which keeps any stabled pony happy.

Changing the diet

Sometimes you have to change a pony's feed, perhaps because he is working harder or you have decided to switch to a different make of food.

Introduce the change gradually, over a week. This gives the pony's digestive system time to adjust.

► **This chart** is a guide only: the *amounts* need to be lessened for a smaller, lighter pony and increased for a larger, heavier one. The *proportions* of hay to short feed, however, apply to all sizes.

Provide both the hay and the short feeds in two lots, giving most at night. For a horse doing hard work, divide the short feed into three portions.

Use dry weights, for example, weigh sugar beet before soaking it. Carrots and apples count as water so don't worry about including their weight in your calculations.

Feed chart for a 350-400 kg. (800-900 lb) pony			
Amount of work	Proportion of hay	Proportion of short feed	Total weight
nil	all	none	7½-10 kg
Light: up to 1 hour a day	9/10	1/10	7½-10 kg
medium: up to 2 hours a day	4/5	1/5	7½-10 kg
hard: up to 3 hours a day	2/3	1/3	7½-10 kg
very hard: hunting, eventing	1/2	1/2	7½-10 kg

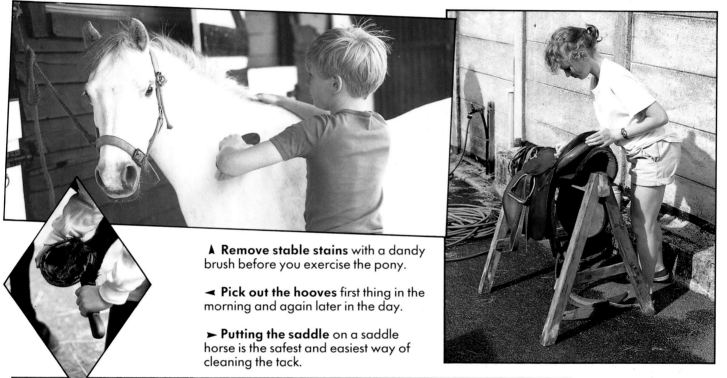

▲ **Remove stable stains** with a dandy brush before you exercise the pony.

◄ **Pick out the hooves** first thing in the morning and again later in the day.

► **Putting the saddle** on a saddle horse is the safest and easiest way of cleaning the tack.

Daily Routine		
Time of day	Duties	Time-saving tips
Before school / work. Allow ½ hour	Change water, muck out, feed, change rugs, pick hooves, give hay	Tie him up outside with his feed so you can muck out quickly and safely
Lunchtime (optional) Allow 15 minutes	Check rugs, water, give hay, skip out	Don't feel guilty if you can't fit this in
After school / work. Allow 1½ hours at least	Quick groom, exercise, change water, rug up, skip out, feed, full groom	If you get home late swap this session with the morning one
Last thing. Allow 15 minutes	Give hay, water, check rugs, skip out	Can be included earlier

◄ **This plan** suggests what chores to do when. Make sure you see to the pony first thing in the morning and in the evening.

The daytime tasks are more flexible, so arrange times that fit in with your other commitments.

Winter stable care

The winter care of a pony kept indoors is one of the most taxing parts of stable management. The pony must have enough exercise and food, and be kept warm, particularly if he is clipped.

Exercise

If you are out most days, the greatest problem is giving the horse enough exercise, as daylight hours are short. The pony must have exercise every day if he is to stay healthy and content, so do your best to get someone else to take him out if you cannot.

At night, if you ride on roads, it is a good idea to wear a stirrup light on your right stirrup. Reflective clothing for yourself and your pony is also safer. Choose the best-lit, quietest roads and avoid dark country lanes or busy main roads. If you have access to a floodlit outdoor arena or an indoor school, this is a great help.

Feeding

Exercise and feeding are closely linked because food supplies the fuel for energy and work. If you can only exercise your pony in the morning or evening, it is best to feed him as much hay as he wants. He may also be better off without any concentrates at all, as long as his bulk food is good quality.

Many ponies can be fed hay *ad lib* (permanently on supply). It is bad management to let ponies get very hungry, which they do when stabled and their hay runs out. This can lead to restlessness, anxiety and stable vices such as wood chewing and crib-biting.

Ponies fed *ad lib* hay do not usually gorge on it as do those only given it twice a day. But if the pony does become very fat, the supply must be restricted.

You can safely ride your pony immediately after he has been eating hay, provided that the exercise is no more demanding than a walk or steady trot. After all, ponies living out eat grass most of the time and move about all the while they are eating. However, if you are going to do faster work such as cantering or jumping, the pony should have no feed for an hour, or slightly longer, before work.

A pony also needs succulent foods in winter, like well-soaked sugar beet pulp, sliced or grated carrots or a whole turnip or mangold (if he likes them). These can be mixed with molassed chop (molasses and chaff) and fed in a bucket or manger, as if they were concentrates.

► **Early morning exercise** can be exhilarating on a crisp winter day and racehorses are galloped daily whatever the weather.

► **Finding time** to exercise a horse can be the most tricky part of winter stable management. You may have to ride at night, in which case make sure you wear light, bright clothing and reflective strips.

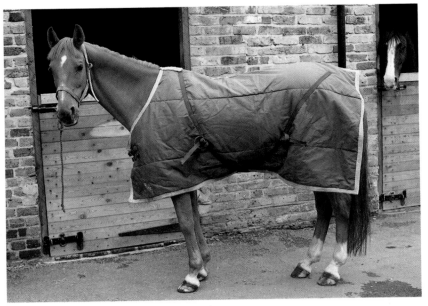

Clipped ponies

An unclipped pony rarely needs a rug —
and one with a breast-and-gullet clip
should only need clothing if he has a
very fine coat due to Arab or Thoroughbred blood. Any pony clipped more than
this needs a rug to help replace his coat.
And, if he has a blanket or hunter clip,
he could need one, or maybe two, under-
rugs or blankets as well.

To check if your pony is cold, feel his
ears, loins and belly in front of his
hindlegs with your bare hands. If he
feels chilly, he needs more clothing, but
don't overload him so that he is uncomfortable and hot.

Modern rugs with criss-cross surcingles are much more comfortable than
the old-fashioned types which are kept
on by a fairly tightly buckled surcingle
or roller round the pony's girth. Such
designs constrict the pony, particularly
when he lies down, and can press on the
spine, causing a sore back and maybe
putting the pony off work.

Unlike traditional jute or wool, modern fabrics are also easily washed. With
any type of rug, however, you really
need two so that you can keep each
properly clean.

Bedding

Bedding should be generous at all times,
but particularly in winter when it also
helps to keep the pony warm. The
warmest beddings are straw and shredded paper, the coldest is peat, and
wood shavings and sawdust come in
between.

Some owners leave a bare patch behind the door so the pony won't drag
bedding out with him, but this may also
leave a draught under the door in
winter. Keep the whole floor bedded

Measuring up for a rug

Any rug should fit from in *front* of the withers, not on top of them — and to the very root of the tail, so that the quarters are fully covered. It should come just past the elbow in depth, to ensure warmth and comfort.

To measure, take a tape measure and start in the *middle* of the pony's breast at the base of his neck. Run it, parallel to the ground, along his side to the back of his thigh. The number of centimetres/inches is the size he takes. You don't need to measure the depth as well: this automatically increases to suit the length.

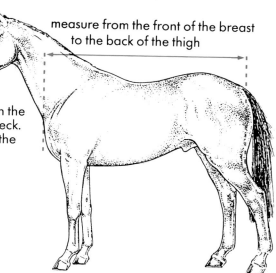

measure from the front of the breast to the back of the thigh

VENTILATION

Do all you can to improve the ventilation of your stable without causing draughts. Ridge roof ventilators or gable-end louvres are an excellent idea, as are windows combined with an open top door.

Always remember to fasten back the door securely so it cannot blow shut on to the pony.

gable-end louvre

ridge roof ventilator

down well and bank up the sides for extra warmth and comfort.

With a pony in all the time, you must remove droppings regularly to keep the bed clean. Even if you keep your pony on deep or semi-deep litter, never leave the yard with droppings in the box. If you possibly can, get someone to skip the stable out when you're not there.

Grooming

Your pony should have a full grooming every day. Because he is not exposed to the rain, which helps clean the coat of an outdoor pony, he has no means of removing the build-up of grease and dandruff in his coat, so you must do it for him.

If you genuinely do not have time, at least sponge his eyes, nostrils, lips, sheath/teats and dock, and under the tail. Dandy brush stable stains and dried mud and sweat, too. This freshens him up until you can do a thorough job.

The most important part of grooming is picking out the feet, particularly with a stabled pony who may often stand in his own droppings. Pick out the feet and check the shoes at least twice a day. Press the frog with the back of your hoof pick. If the pony flinches, it could mean he has thrush developing: this may occur on damp, dirty bedding. If there is also a nasty smell and maybe a dark discharge from the frog, call the vet at once.

Ventilation

Clean, fresh air is essential for ponies, who were born to live outside and cannot bear muggy, stuffy air – they can stand almost any amount of dry, still, cold air.

What they hate is wind and wet, particularly combined. Never shut the top door of your pony's stable unless the wind and rain are blowing directly in and, even then, leave the window open. Ideally, there should also be a window on the opposite side of the box, so you can leave that open when it is on the sheltered side in a lashing storm.

◄ **Picking out** the hooves every day is vital. Neglecting the feet can mean the pony develops unpleasant diseases such as thrush.

Exercise plans for a . . .

. . . stable-kept pony

A stabled pony doing up to 1½ hours' work four or five times a week can be described as half fit. This is enough for normal hacking, light schooling, a little jumping and the occasional dressage test or showing class. If you are planning to do more energetic work with your pony – such as hunting, long-distance riding or sponsored rides – you need to increase his level of fitness.

Stabling over grass

A grass-kept pony can only ever be half fit. This is because he spends much of the time with a full belly. A pony's stomach lies very close to his lungs, and a full stomach limits the lungs' ability to inflate during hard work. Eating a lot of bulk food means the pony requires more space in his abdomen, and slows him down in hard work.

A stable-kept pony can have his rations reduced before work so that his lungs can work fully. By reducing the amount of bulk he eats, the size of his belly can also be limited.

Remember, though, that a stabled pony is unable to walk about as much as the pony who is kept at grass. This lack of natural freedom must be compensated for by regular, controlled exercise. A whole day without going out of the stable will leave your pony feeling stiff, uncomfortable and probably explosive!

Exercise and work

Exercise and work are not always the same. A 'free' pony can 'exercise' himself as and when he feels in the mood. He moves about gently most of the time. Work, however, involves exercising, often strenuously, for *controlled* periods of time.

During training, certain groups of muscles are developed, lung and heart capacity is increased and limbs are toughened. *Exercise* is important for general circulation and well being. *Work* is important for the special demands made on riding ponies, so that they can do the job asked of them easily and without strain.

◄ **Hillwork** increases the pony's stamina. Remember to lean forward slightly so that you take the weight off the pony's back, and keep him to a steady pace.

TIME AND MOTION TIPS

If you are out all day it can be hard to find time for exercising your pony as well as doing stable chores. When this is the case, follow these tips:

● Do faster work on your busy days and longer rides at weekends.

● Teach a friend how to lunge for the days when your time is short.

● Ask someone else to give him a lunchtime feed, part concentrates, part hay.

● If you have the chance to turn him out, use a New Zealand rug to keep him warm and dry.

Ponies and personality

In making a pony extra fit, allowances must be made for each pony's individual progress. A lively pony that has previously been fit, takes less time to bring to full fitness than a lazy pony. The longer a pony has been in light work only, the greater time you should allow for him to reach a peak.

It also depends on the rider: an athletic pony with a capable rider progresses better than a short-striding, heavily built pony with a novice rider.

With this in mind, the programme here is an approximate guide for an average pony of around 14 hands high.

Watchpoints

As you work toward fitness, watch these points.

● **Sweating:** A fit pony's sweat is clean and dries quickly. An unfit pony sheds a lot of grease and grime as he sweats. This makes him lather up, feel sticky and dry off slowly.

● **Fat or muscle:** Fat is flabby, soft and prone to dimples. Muscle is smoother, firmer to touch and can be seen to contract or extend as the pony moves.

● **Breathing:** Unfit ponies breathe with quick, shallow movements. After work, the rapid breathing may go on for some time. A fit pony takes deeper, more

◄ **Flatwork** can be increased in the fourth week. Trotting in circles, serpentines or figures of eight is good for balance and discipline.

▼ **Cantering** during schooling should be controlled and to a plan – you, and not the pony, must decide on the direction and speed.

rhythmical breaths and recovers in a few minutes after stopping work.

● **Skin and hair:** A fit pony is sleeker, shinier and cleaner than his unfit counterpart. He is also more sensitive during grooming, while the unfit pony enjoys a good scratch!

Nobody should know more about your pony than you who sees him every day. Take note of even the slightest change. It is better to hold up your programme by a week than to lose six months because your pony has gone lame. A steady improvement should be obvious and is your guide to move on to the next stage of the programme.

▲ **Jumping** logs across the path when out hacking stops your pony becoming stale from too much schooling.

► **Work at home** can include jumping as well as flatwork throughout the programme. Trotting poles and small fences are valuable for training at any level.

The fitness programme

Starting point: Walk, trot, canter, occasional short gallop, some jumping. One or two days off per week.
Feeding: Total of 2.7kg (6lbs) concentrates, 5.5kg (12lbs) hay split into two, the evening feed larger than the morning one. The concentrates can be made up from any of the following: pony nuts, bran (not more than ¼kg/½lb), flaked barley, sugar beet pulp, plus cut-up apple or carrot, for example. If you use a 'mix', check the ingredients to see what the proportion of oats is.

Week 1–2: Aim to work six days a week, for about 1–1½ hours per day. Increase walking to tone up muscles and harden limbs. Include some roadwork. Walk up and down hills without change of rhythm.
Feeding: Add ½kg (1lb) oats to evening feed after working days, plus ½kg other concentrates if the pony is losing condition. Remember that fat is a hindrance but food replaces lost energy.

Week 2–3: On two days a week, increase fast work. After a short gallop, continue in slow canter and follow with second short gallop. You are now working on heart and lung capacity.
Feeding: Gradually increase the oat ration unless the pony is already too lively. Boiled or flaked barley is then a good substitute. Reduce the hay by ½–1kg (1–2lbs).

Week 4–5: Continue with fast work twice a week, and with walking exercise. Increase time spent schooling at home, flat or jumping.
Feeding: Carefully increase oat ration, but only if it's justified by performance and condition. One day per week, a mash can be given. This should be the night before exercising — as opposed to working — only.

Week 5–6: If possible, increase time on slow days to 2½–3 hours including walking in and cooling off. Jumping performance should now be almost to competition level. Include sustained half-speed work — a moderately brisk canter for up to 3.2km (2 miles).
Feeding: Continue to increase as before. Total concentrates are now about 4.5kg (10lbs). If work is light on any day, or if the pony is too frisky, reduce the concentrate and replace with hay.

Week 7: Leave at least two days between fast, hard, training work and competition. 1½ hours' walking and steady trotting the day before keeps the pony fresh but not stiff.
Feeding: The pony should be eating the same amount of concentrated and bulk feed, about 10–11kg (20–22lbs) in all, depending on his weight and particular needs.

Waiting expectantly for his feed-time

The combined system

Keeping your pony on a combined system means he is partly stabled and partly turned out at grass. It is an excellent method that gives the pony the best of both worlds.

How the system works

The pony spends part of each 24 hours stabled and part at grass, although he may also have the occasional day entirely in or out. The system is very flexible, and you make of it exactly what you want. The time stabled or out depends entirely on what suits you and your pony's routine: there are no hard and fast rules.

Generally, the pony might spend the days out in winter and be stabled at night, so that when the temperature drops overnight he has the warmth and comfort of his stable. In the summer, he can be turned out in the cooler evening and be stabled during the day, away from the sun and the flies.

You can tailor the pony's hours in and out to your own requirements. If you are going to a summer show, for instance, you may want to keep him in the night beforehand so he stays clean.

When you do change the routine, make sure the pony has a daily supply of all his normal food — grass, hay and whatever else he usually has as well as water — so his digestion can cope. Where people go wrong with the combined system is in not keeping to the usual feeding routine, which thoroughly upsets the pony and can make him ill.

In winter, particularly if you tend to work your pony fairly hard at weekends and he is clipped, he can spend his days out wearing a New Zealand rug. You could go to the stables in the morning, ride or not as you wish, feed and brush him over, then turn him out for the day. He should have a good hay supply in the paddock to make up for the winter grass which has very little goodness in it.

▼ **For special occasions,** you can wash a combined-system pony as long as you thoroughly rinse and dry him afterwards.

If you make a habit of washing him — before weekend shows, for example — do not body brush the pony during the week. Quartering with the dandy brush (inset) is enough. As the pony is out for much of the time, he needs the protection of some natural grease in his coat.

◄ **A comforting routine:** These riding school ponies are usually kept in a field at night and stabled by day. They are so familiar with their daily schedule that they trot from field to stable every morning as soon as the gate is opened. Each pony knows that, once he is in the stable (inset), a feed is about to appear!

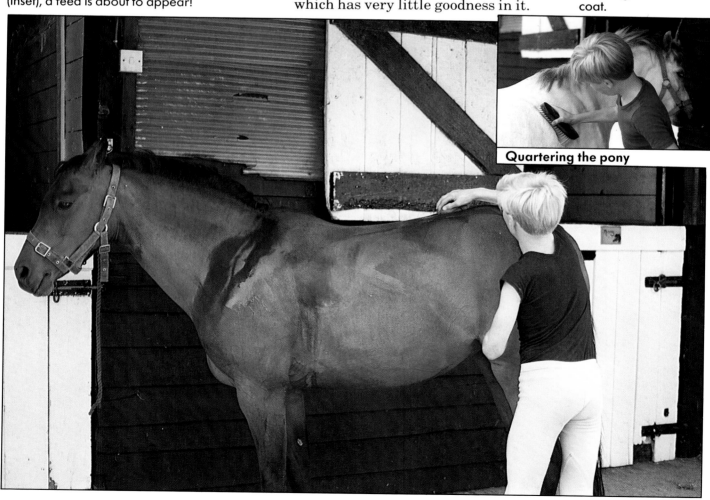

Quartering the pony

► **Feeding:** If several of you keep your ponies at DIY livery, you can arrange a rota to save time. Take it in turns to do morning chores such as mixing up the feeds.

Although the combined system is flexible, it is important to stick to a regular feeding pattern, or your pony may get colic.

▲ **Freedom to play:** A pony that's stabled for part of the time appreciates the open spaces of a field.

► **Mucking out:** One drawback of the combined system is that you have to do stable and field chores. As well as mucking out and keeping the yard tidy, you need to check the field regularly and remove droppings from the pasture.

But the good points outweigh the bad: the pony requires less exercising and leads a more natural life than a stabled horse.

Share with friends

If you keep the pony at a do-it-yourself livery yard, you can work out a rota with friends to share the chores so you do not have to go to the yard twice, or even once, every day.

However, you do all have to be trustworthy and knowledgeable enough so that, if one of you spots something wrong with a friend's pony, you can ring and tell the owner. You each have to treat the other ponies as if they were your own and look after them properly when it is your turn.

Obviously, one person cannot possibly exercise more than one pony early in the morning. But he or she could easily feed and turn out two friends' ponies, or bring them in if it is summer, and exercise their own pony. Exact rotas can be worked out and set down in a diary or on a wall chart, so everyone knows what they are supposed to be doing. If someone is sick, they ring up and someone else takes over their rota.

You have to use your common sense and co-operate with each other, but such systems work very well if everyone concerned is sensible and responsible and does the tasks allotted to them.

Day-to-day care

As far as grooming goes, combined system ponies can be groomed as for stabled ponies. But if they are going to be out *without* New Zealand rugs in winter, they should not be body brushed. This is because, when out for a lot of the time, horses need some natural grease in their coats for protection. And remember that the pony must have some sort of field shelter, even if only straw bales inside a framework.

It is still a good idea to use an effective fly repellant on a combined system pony in summer. Night-flying insects can be just as much of a nuisance as the daytime ones.

The advantages

From the pony's point of view, the combined system is ideal. He has the shelter and peace of his stable, if that is what he wants. Yet he also has freedom to play about as he wishes when out and, if he is kept with other ponies, the company of his friends in the field.

From your point of view, the beauty of this system is that you do not *have* to ride the pony if the weather is dreadful or you are busy. He exercises himself in the field, particularly if he has company and is warm and well fed.

Two such ponies, or more, out together, keep themselves half fit, so you only really have to ride them on two or maybe three days during the week, to ensure that they are toned up for work at weekends.

However, because both field and stable are involved, you do have the double job of checking the fencing and general condition of the field and also mucking out the stable and doing other indoor chores. But this is barely noticeable with the amount of time that you save on exercising.

Overall, the combined system is probably the best and most convenient form of management both for you and your pony. It allows you to keep him fitter and cleaner than a grass-kept pony yet still gives the pony freedom and a relatively natural lifestyle.

Yarding

Yarding is a system of keeping horses and ponies in a surfaced yard or enclosure. They are out in the open, if they want to be, yet are not at grass, so you can regulate their feeding.

The best yards have a covered area so the animals can wander in and out as they wish. Often a large barn-type building is used with a wide entrance. The ground surface of the covered area can be of normal bedding, as in a field shelter or stable. The pony should be fed with hay and succulents to compensate for the lack of grass. A water supply of some kind is essential.

The ground surface of the outside area must be safe and non-slip so the ponies can canter about and play around just as when in a field. Usually the materials are wood-chip based, perhaps with sand and salt added — rather like the materials used to floor indoor schools or outdoor arenas.

The fencing around the yard is ideally wooden post and rail. But any normal, safe fencing material recommended for horses — such as smooth, taut wire — is acceptable.

The pony should be treated like a combined system-kept animal. Although it may not be as carefree as a proper field, a yard is certainly more relaxing for a pony than being stabled for too long. Yards are particularly useful when the weather is so bad that turning out is impractical — in deep snow or if the paddock is waterlogged — and horses can happily live in such conditions all the year round.

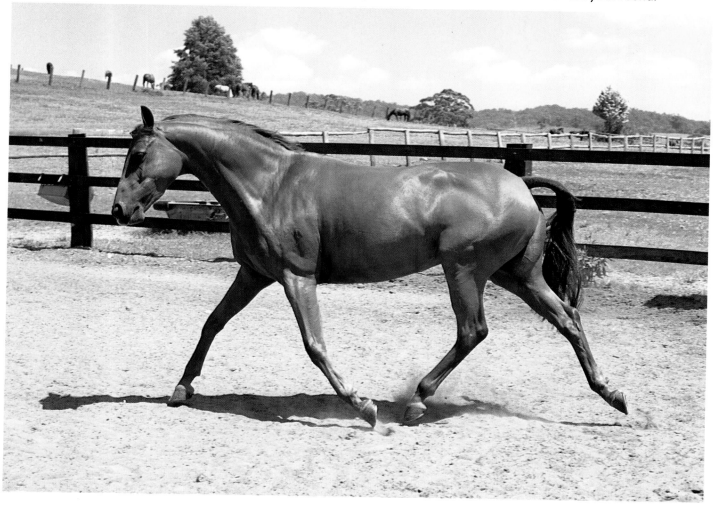

Rugs for the stable

You may wonder why ponies need rugs at all when they have natural fur coats to keep them warm. The answer is that unclipped ponies kept outside *are* less likely to need rugs.

But once a stabled pony is clipped – to stop him sweating too much during work and catching a chill afterwards – he feels the cold. When kept inside he is usually groomed to remove grease and can't trot about to keep warm. If ponies get cold, they need more food, catch more illnesses and feel miserable.

▼ A modern stable rug is the most important choice for a stabled pony. If you are only buying one rug, this cosy quilted 'anorak' will keep any pony snug throughout the winter. Synthetic stable rugs are also washable.

Indoor rugs

There are many different rugs for wearing in the stable, and all serve different purposes. The most important one, and the only one you need to begin with, is the stable rug.

Modern stable rugs are quilted and very warm and snug – like a pony anorak. They are made of easy-care, synthetic fabrics and so are quick to launder. Ponies can wear them night and day in winter – so a good stable rug is the basis of their wardrobe.

Anti-sweat rugs are like string vests. They are usually placed under an ordinary rug, where they trap air next to the coat, helping to dry off a pony wet from sweat or rain.

Day rugs are smart woollen rugs bound with cotton braid and often bearing your initials or the pony's name. They have to be dry cleaned and so are for daytime wear when the pony is unlikely to lie on a dirty bed.

Night rugs, of jute and often lined with wool, are worn at night when the pony might lie on his bedding.

Summer sheets are just to keep the dust and flies off a groomed, stabled pony in summer. They are made of cotton or linen, are fairly easy to launder, and can be worn night or day.

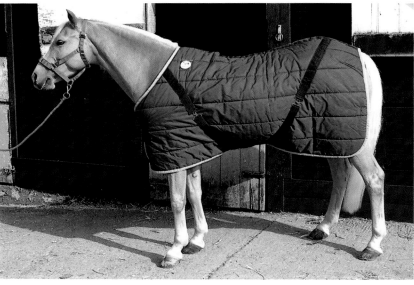

🐎 KEEP OUT THE COLD

Always keep a rug handy in case of sickness, when a pony can feel chilly even in summer. Although a healthy, unclipped pony can manage all year round without any, he may get soaking wet. When he's drenched, a rug helps to dry him off more quickly, so avoiding chills.

However, don't *over*-rug a pony – he'll be uncomfortable. Feel under the rug; if he's sweating he's too hot! But when his loins and the base of his ears are cold, he'll feel cold all over.

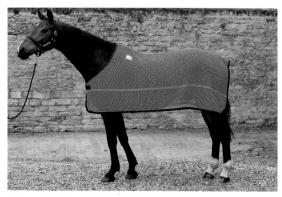

▲ **Anti-sweat rug**

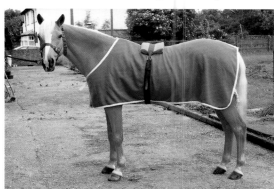

▲ **Day rug**

▲ **Night rug**

▲ **Summer sheet**

Rugging up

Before rugging up it is important to make sure that the pony's rug fits snugly. The best rugs have cross-surcingles (diagonal side-straps) which readjust as the pony moves, rather than a single belt around the pony's middle.

Fitting a rug

To work out what size rug a pony needs, measure him from the mid-point of his chest — where the front buckles fasten — to the furthest point on the back of his quarters — where the fillet string goes. Once you have this measurement, a good saddler can advise you on the correct-sized rug — 158cm (5ft 3in) is about right for a 13.2-hand pony.

A rug which is too large slips back behind the withers, making the pony's withers and shoulders sore. And if a rug is too small, it also rubs and leaves the quarters partly uncovered.

How to put a rug on

1 Fold the rug in half bringing the back over to the front. Approach the pony's near-side shoulder to let him know you are there and pat him gently. Quietly throw the rug over the pony with the front of it well forward from the withers.

2 Unfold the rug down the pony's back and over his quarters. Straighten it so that the centre seam runs down the spine. If the rug is too far forward pull it toward the pony's tail. Avoid moving the rug the other way — toward the withers — as this makes the hair lie in the wrong direction, and is uncomfortable.

3 Fasten the cross-surcingle around the pony's middle first. This ensures that the rug stays in place even if the pony moves off. If you do up the front fastenings first and the pony shifts position the rug can twist around and end up like a bib, over his front legs.

4 Move to the front of the rug and fasten the buckles across the breast. Check that the rug fits loosely in front of the shoulder so that the pony can move freely.

5 Standing to one side of the pony's quarters — the correct position to avoid being kicked — do up the buckle at the back of the rug under the pony's tail, and then the fillet string. If the string is too long when you fit the rug for the first time, cut off any excess. But make sure you leave enough to secure the rug properly.

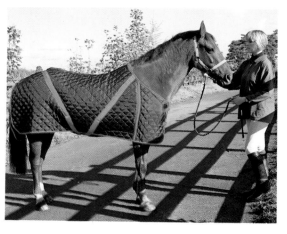

6 Now your rug should be fitted comfortably and securely.
When taking it off, begin by undoing the buckle at the back (if there is one), then undo the front, and finally the cross-surcingle. You can leave the fillet string done up. By working in this order, the rug stays safely in place if the pony moves.

5 Grooming

Grooming a grass-kept pony

The great bonus about a grass-kept pony is that you don't have much grooming to do. In fact, 'outdoor' ponies must not be kept as clean as stabled ones because they need some natural grease to help protect them against the weather.

❗ WET PONIES
● In wet weather there may always be some powdery mud left in the coat. This doesn't matter and you can't do anything about it except wash the pony (not advised in winter).

Never brush wet mud as you'll just push it through to the skin. Dry the pony first by thatching him (see illustration opposite).

Why groom?

Why do ponies need grooming? After all, those running wild aren't groomed. No, but the dirt in their coats often attracts lice and ticks which suck blood and cause sore skin.

As well as helping a pony to look nice and feel better – grooming is like a form of massage – brushing the coat also removes most of the dust and dirt. This means you can check for parasites and wounds which could become infected if left.

You need to remove mud from the pony's coat, prevent his mane and tail from becoming tangled, pick out dirt from his hooves and sponge sensitive parts such as eyes and dock (under the tail).

The basic kit

The basic grooming kit for a grass-kept pony includes a hoof pick (a metal hook to remove dirt from the underside of the hooves), a dandy brush (which has longish, stiff bristles for brushing off dried mud and loose hairs), a rubber or plastic curry comb (for removing caked-on mud), two sponges (one for his head and the other for his back end) and a bucket of water. Use differently coloured sponges so that you don't muddle them.

Useful extras are a body brush and a water brush. Body brushes have short, close bristles for getting through a summer coat to the skin, but don't use them in winter. A water brush is a smaller version of a dandy brush, with soft bristles for use on the mane, forelock and tail.

How to groom

You should groom a grass-kept pony *before* riding to make him look respectable and to stop mud on the saddle and bridle areas chafing the skin. Go through the basic routine every day if possible, winter and summer, and always before working him. It takes about half an hour, less as you get used to it. If you haven't time for a full groom, at least pick out the feet and sponge daily.

Tie your pony up with a quick-release knot. If you're outdoors, face him to the wind so dirt doesn't blow back on to cleaned parts or in your face.

First pick out the hooves, paying special attention to the sides and cleft (middle groove) of the frog. With the

The equipment you need

The essentials for grooming a grass-kept pony are a hoof pick; *either* a rubber curry comb *or* a plastic one; a dandy brush; two sponges (different colours help you to keep them separate); and a bucket full of clean water.

Useful but not essential are a body brush and water brush for the head, mane and tail. Never use the body brush on a winter coat — you remove all the natural grease that protects a grass-kept pony from cold, wet weather.

body brush

dandy brush

bucket

two sponges

hoof pick

rubber curry comb

water brush

plastic curry comb

curry comb, carefully scrub off all dirt that's caked on your pony's body. Take the dandy brush and, working in the direction the hair grows, brush the pony firmly but not roughly. Start at the front and work back and down so you don't brush dirt on to parts already done. Be gentle on the head, where it is advisable to use the softer body brush.

Try this routine so you don't miss anywhere: head, left side of the neck, under the neck, the breast and between forelegs, shoulder, foreleg, back, quarters, side, flank, under the girth area and belly and lastly the hindleg. Repeat on the right side. Remove all dried-on mud and sweat from the saddle and bridle area before tacking up.

Forelock, mane and tail

These are done with the body brush, if you have one or, gently, to avoid breaking the hairs, with the dandy brush or dry water brush. Use your fingers to untangle knots.

To groom the tail, put your hand round all the hair at the end of the dock and hold it straight out toward you. Letting a few hairs fall down, brush them out starting at the bottom and working up to the roots. Gradually let down all the long strands, then separate the shorter hair at the top of the dock to get at the roots.

Lift the forelock with one hand, and brush out from the roots a few hairs at a time. Now push the mane over to the 'wrong' side of the neck and, starting behind the ears, brush it back over, lock by lock, from the roots.

Thatching

Before grooming a wet pony you need to dry him off by 'thatching' him. Pile a thick layer of straw on his back, fasten on a rug (inside out so you don't get straw on the lining) and leave him tied up, preferably in a stable, until he's dry. This could take up to two hours with a long winter coat.

If you have no straw, use an anti-sweat rug or an old cotton-mesh bed blanket instead.

Sponging

Take your 'head' sponge and wet it, squeezing it well until just damp. Gently sponge dirt and discharge from the eyes, inside the nostrils and the lips, steadying the pony's head with your hand.

Damp the 'back end' sponge and clean the sheath (if the pony is a gelding) or udder (if a mare), under the tail and between the buttocks. In cold weather, dry sponged parts with an old towel as the pony could get chapped skin if they are left damp.

And that's it!

Tying up

Tie the pony in a safe place — stable, yard or field.

Use a quick-release knot which can be undone, in emergency, with one tug on the free end. It is safest to tie up to a string loop which breaks if the pony pulls back in fright. The tying point should be as high as his head, if possible, to prevent him getting his legs caught up in the rope.

1 Loop the rope through the safety string.

2 Use the end of the loop to form a bow.

3 Pull the bow tight to fasten the pony securely.

4 Pass the loose end through the bow so it can't be undone.

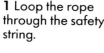
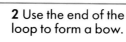

1 Pick any stones, dirt and mud out of the hooves, always working methodically from heel to toe.

2 Make sure the pony is facing into the wind before using a plastic (or rubber) curry comb to remove caked mud.

5 Use a body brush to comb the tail, working through a few strands at a time.

6 Push the mane to the other side and brush it back over, starting behind the ears.

7 Dampen one sponge, wring out excess water, and remove dirt and discharge from the nostrils, eyes and lips.

8 Clean the dock with the other sponge. In cold weather, dry sponged parts with a towel to prevent chapped skin.

3 Finish cleaning the coat with the dandy brush, working from the front down toward the back.

4 Move calmly behind the pony to untangle the worst tail knots with your fingers.

Now you're ready to ride!

Grooming a stabled pony

WISPING

Nowadays most people use a leather massage pad for wisping. But grooms used to wisp with hay.

To make a wisp, twist damp hay tightly into a 'rope' 2m (6½ft) long.

Form two loops at one end and twist the rest tightly round them.

Tuck the loose end firmly under the last twist.

17·5cm (7in)

The basic grooming routine for grass-kept ponies is also used for stabled ponies, but for these there are two other parts of the process. The first, body brushing, is essential; the second, wisping (toning the muscles), is a matter of choice.

A full grooming

Stabled ponies need a full daily grooming unless some emergency prevents it. As they do not stand out in the rain, they have no need of their natural grease for protection. So body brushing keeps them clean.

Grass-kept ponies often roll to stimulate their skin and to massage their muscles. Stabled ponies are more restricted, so wisping helps to replace the benefits of rolling.

Equipment

You need all the basics used for a grass-kept pony – hoof pick, dandy brush, rubber or plastic curry comb, two sponges and a bucket of water – plus a few more.

The body brush is essential now. You also need a metal curry comb to clean it. Use a stable rubber (like a tea towel) or sponge for a final polish, and a hay wisp or a leather massage pad for wisping.

Don't use mane combs in grooming because they break the hairs. They are for trimming the mane (shortening and thinning it).

Hoof oils only do the pony any good if they contain hoof conditioner and/or antiseptic, but they do give a smart and shiny appearance. Ask your farrier for advice on this.

Quartering

After the pony's morning feed he is quartered. This means you fold his rugs back off the front of his body and dandy brush over both sides to remove stable stains. Fold the rugs forward and do the back half so all four 'quarters' of the body are tidied ready for work.

Quickly brush the mane and tail with the body brush so there is no bedding in them, and pick out the feet. Quartering takes about ten minutes.

Strapping

After work you should groom the pony fully (called strapping) while his skin is warm but dry and easier to clean. First, pick out his feet again, then dandy brush him all over as for a grass-kept pony to remove dirt.

Now take your body brush in one hand and your metal curry comb in the other. Slot your hand through the wide loop on the back of the brush with your thumb on the outside to hold it firm. If doing the left side use your left arm for the brush, and vice versa.

Hold your arm stiff but slightly bent, and run the brush along the pony's neck by leaning your *weight* on to it to push the bristles through to the skin. Make long, curved strokes.

If you push with your *arm* rather than letting your weight do the work you get

---

▼ **A full grooming kit:** As well as the basic equipment you need a body brush and a metal curry comb. Use a stable rubber for polishing and a wisp or leather massage pad for toning the muscles.

stable rubber

dandy brush

body brush

leather massage pad

rubber curry comb

water brush

metal curry combs   hoof pick

tired before the pony is finished and end up only half doing the job. If your arm does get tired, use the other one for a while. Six brush strokes in one place should be enough.

After two or three strokes, hold the bristles downward on top of the teeth of the curry comb and drag them firmly across it to clean them. Every now and then, tap the curry comb on its side on the floor (near the door if you're inside the stable) to dislodge the dirt.

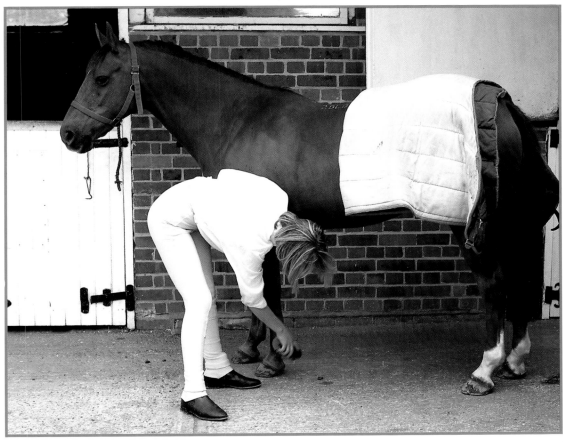

◄ **Quartering** is a ten-minute clean-up done in the morning after 'breakfast' and before exercise. Go over the pony's coat with the dandy brush to get rid of stable stains. Keep the pony's rug folded over the half you are *not* brushing so he stays warm.

When you've brushed the coat, switch to the body brush and remove any bedding from mane and tail, then pick out the feet.

◄ **Strapping** requires plenty of hard work. You should use the body brush after exercise when the pony is warm to clean the coat and massage the skin. Go gently on the legs and head.

▲ **Clean the brush** every few strokes by dragging the bristles through the teeth of the curry comb. *Never* use a metal curry comb on a pony — its *only* use is to remove dirt from the brush.

▲ **Remove dirt** from the curry comb by tapping it on the ground. Do this down wind of the pony so dirt doesn't blow back over him, and well away from his legs so you don't get kicked.

Brush thoroughly all over the coat.

On delicate parts (like head and legs) do not lean with your weight or use long strokes; just press on and brush in the direction of the hair. If your pony dislikes having his head brushed, use the stable rubber.

Body brushing is hard work and, if you're not used to it, could well take you half an hour.

After body brushing, do the forelock, mane and tail as for a grass-kept pony, and 'lay' them with the damp water brush. Sponge the eyes, nostrils, lips and dock and, finally, damp the stable rubber slightly, bundle it up and wipe over the coat.

Now the pony is finished – and you're exhausted!

▲ **Brush the head very gently.** Take the headcollar off and strap it round the pony's neck so you can reach every part. Some ponies object to having their heads brushed – if so, use a stable rubber instead.

◄ **Flattening the mane:** After brushing the mane with the body brush, take the water brush and dip the ends of the bristles in water. Shake them hard downward and brush the hair flat.

▼ **Polishing** finishes the grooming session. Damp a stable rubber (either a clean tea towel or a sponge does the job if you don't have one). Scrunch it up into a bundle and wipe lightly all over the coat.

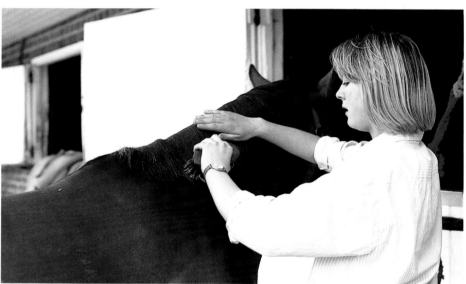

Do's and don'ts

☐ DON'T brush wet mud – it won't come off and you'll make the pony sore. Either hose it off or wait until the pony is dry, then brush it off.

☐ DON'T tug the brush through tangles in the mane or tail because you'll break the hair. Use your fingers.

☐ DON'T be rough or knock the pony with your tools while you groom.

☐ DO be considerate so the pony enjoys being groomed.

☐ DO pick out the feet at least twice daily for a stabled pony.

☐ DO speak kindly to the pony while grooming – then he'll respond to you.

To keep a stable-kept pony in tip-top condition, give him a full daily grooming. He can enjoy the massage while you make him clean and trim.

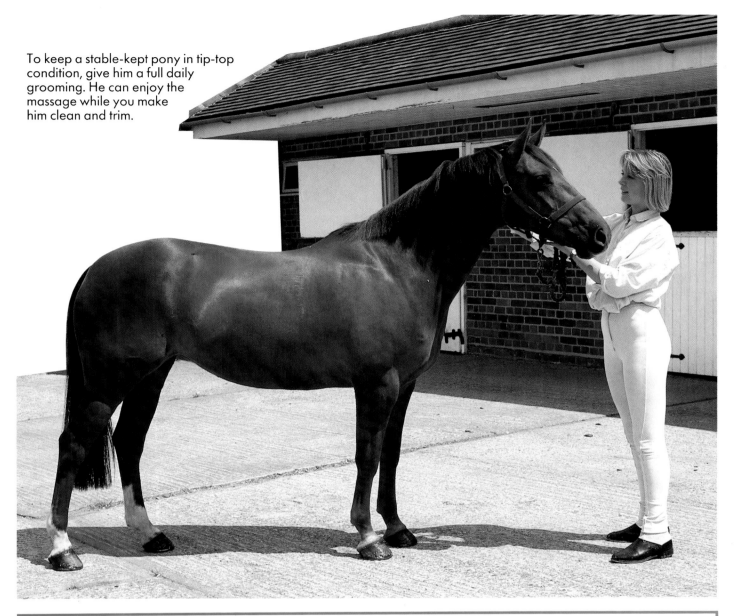

Setting fair and wisping

In the evening, go quickly over the pony with the body brush (known as brushing over or setting fair), and perhaps wisp him. Alternatively, you can wisp in the morning after body brushing. Most ponies enjoy having their muscles toned.

To wisp, use your weight in long strokes as in body brushing, and slap the wisp or massage pad firmly — but not *too* hard! — on to the top half of the neck, shoulders and quarters.

Don't wisp other parts, especially the loins (behind the saddle area) or legs as you could cause injury.

The idea is that the pony, expecting the slap, flinches his muscles to brace himself against the force. This helps to develop his muscles. Ten minutes each side is plenty.

areas to wisp

Hoof care

Whether a pony is kept at grass or in a stable, his feet need daily attention to keep them clean and healthy.

Picking up the feet

Before checking your pony's feet, tie him up securely so that he can't move around. Always attend to him quietly as this relaxes him. Make sure he is standing square with his weight evenly distributed on all four feet.

Starting with the near fore (left foreleg), stand facing the pony's tail. Run your left hand down his leg so he realizes you are going to do something to him. If you suddenly grab his foot you could frighten him.

Most ponies lift their foot as soon as your hand reaches the pastern (just above the hoof and below the fetlock joint). If yours doesn't respond, firmly pinch his pastern with your thumb and index finger.

Picking out

You should pick out your pony's feet at least once and preferably twice a day. When you've lifted the near fore, rest it in your left hand and hold the hoof pick in your right. You'll have to bend or crouch down but *never* kneel or sit. You must be able to get out of the way quickly if the pony is unexpectedly startled.

Gently pick out any mud, rubbish and grit. Always work from the heel toward the toe – never the other direction. This way, there is no possibility of pushing a piece of grit into the sensitive part of the frog by the bars.

Pick out each foot in turn, near fore, near hind, off fore and off hind.

Washing the feet

To wash away all traces of dirt from the hoof use a water brush dipped into a bucket of water. Shake off any excess water. If your hoof pick has a brush attachment, you can use that instead.

Wash out the underside of the foot in the same direction as you use the hoof pick – working from heel to toe. Don't let water run into his heel as this can cause 'cracked heels' – like chapped hands for us. Place your thumb across the heel if you're splashing water, and never use a drenched, soaking brush.

Put your pony's foot down and wash the wall of the hoof. Take care not to go above the hoof wall.

Hoof oil

When the feet are dry, you can put on a thin coating of hoof oil. There are special brushes for this, but a small, clean 2–2.5cm (1in) paint brush does the job just as well. Oil the whole of the hoof, inside and out, including the bulbs of the heel. Do the inside first so *you* don't get smothered in oil.

Whether hoof oil does the feet good is a matter of dispute. But it makes the hooves gleam, and is generally beneficial for ponies with broken or brittle feet. Some also contain antiseptic, which helps ward off infections.

◄ **Gleaming shiny hooves** add greatly to a smart appearance.

Pick out your pony's hooves every day to get rid of manure, mud and stones. Washing and oiling can be done less often.

Know the foot

The frog is 'V'-shaped and provides the foot with a natural non-slip shock absorber.
The sole protects the underside of the foot. This is fairly thin, more so with some ponies than others, which is why you should take care when riding over a stony surface.
The wall is the most visible part of the hoof. Although it is continually growing it is insensitive. Compare it with our own finger or toe nails which have no feeling but still grow.

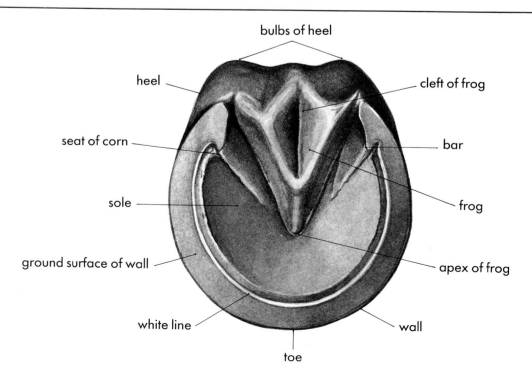

bulbs of heel

heel — cleft of frog

seat of corn — bar

sole — frog

ground surface of wall — apex of frog

white line — wall

toe

hoof oil

hoof oil
brush

water
brush

hoof picks

Regular check-ups

Remember to get your pony's feet regularly attended to by a farrier. A horse should have his shoes checked every three to five weeks, depending on the amount of road work you are doing and how often you ride.

Even an unshod horse needs five-weekly check-ups because the hoof wall grows non-stop – he needs his nails cut!

Causes of lameness

Ponies often become lame if a stone lodges between the shoe and the frog. This usually happens while you are riding – you suddenly feel your pony falter. Dismount immediately and pick out his foot gently. You can buy portable folding hoof picks; otherwise use your finger or a strong stick.

Nails in the feet are also common.

The complete treatment

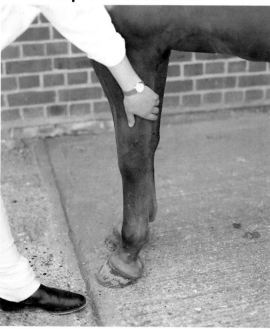

1 Facing the tail, run your left hand smoothly down the pony's leg to warn him you're going to pick his foot up.

2 Hold the hoof in your left hand and, with the hoof pick in your right hand, remove dirt and grit. Work from heel to toe.

▲ Your hoof-care kit should contain a hoof pick, water brush for washing (an old dandy brush will do), hoof oil and a brush.

5 Oil the inside of the hoof thoroughly, working it well in to the sole, frog and heel and all the crevices.

6 Put a light coat of oil on the hoof wall, starting at the top and taking care to avoid dirtying the hair above.

Before you remove a nail note whereabouts it is, what angle it is at and how deeply it has gone in. The nail may be penetrating a vital structure if it is in the back third of the foot or frog, in which case call the vet.

Thrush is a fungus and also needs the attention of a vet. It appears in the cleft of the hoof and gives off a foul smell like bad cheese. Its discharge is easily seen and occurs if you do not clean the pony's feet regularly or you leave him standing in a dirty stable.

Laminitis has many known causes, one of which is eating too much lush grass. Typically, the pony is in considerable pain, unable to walk properly and his feet feel hot to the touch. It is very serious and should always receive prompt veterinary action.

3 Dampen the water brush and use it to get rid of the last traces of dirt, but don't slosh water over the heel!

4 Put the hoof down and crouch to brush any mud off the outside of the hoof wall, keeping water away from the hair.

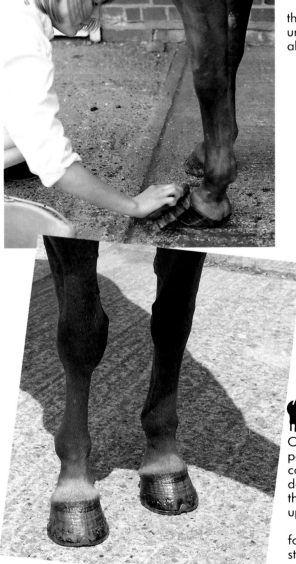

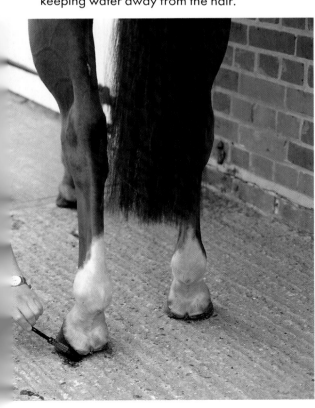

7 The reward of your daily foot treatment is knowing that the pony in your care has four hooves glistening with health and strength!

! HORSE CHESTNUT

If a pony is really stubborn and won't lift his foot up even when you pinch his pastern, there's a last resort.

Twist his chestnut (the horny piece just above the knee) with one hand while holding on to his foot with the other.

This is painful for the pony so don't do it unless you are absolutely desperate.

THE NEAR SIDE

Once you and your pony have confidence, you can do all the hooves from the near side to speed up hoof care.

To reach the off fore and off hind, you stretch underneath the pony and just run your left hand down his leg and quietly pick it up.

Shoeing

To protect your pony's feet and stop them becoming sore and broken when you ride him, you need to have him shod.

What are shoes?

Shoes are made up from lengths of iron or from steel. These vary in width and depth depending on the size of the horse and what kind of work he does.

Your pony will probably be fitted with a lightweight shoe, unless he has a foot problem – in which case the farrier may use a special shoe to try to remedy the fault.

An ordinary front shoe has a front toe clip, which helps to hold the shoe in place, and usually seven nail holes. There is often a groove which runs round the centre of the shoe. This is called fullering and gives the shoe better grip when it comes into contact with the ground. A hind shoe is similar except that it has two toe clips placed either side of the toe of the shoe.

The farrier

You may have heard the terms farrier and blacksmith used. Both shoe horses and deal with diseases of the hoof. But a blacksmith also carries out welding and other metalwork, which is useful if you need any stable fittings made or mended. Their apprenticeships are four and five years respectively.

The work a farrier does is very skilled, and its important to get a good recommendation before making a choice. Your vet may be able to suggest the name of a good farrier.

Nowadays most farriers have mobile forges, so if you live far away they can come to you. However, it's cheaper if you go to their premises – you don't have to pay their travelling fee on top of the price of fitting a set of shoes.

Do make sure you book regular appointments. Arrive on time at the forge or have the pony caught up ready when the farrier arrives. Have the legs as clean and dry as possible.

Remember that day-to-day foot care is your responsibility – the farrier can't make good feet from bad at one shoeing. Pick the feet out daily, oiling them if necessary, and feed the pony properly so as to build good horn.

What the farrier does

There are two main methods of shoeing: 'hot' and 'cold'.

Hot shoeing is when the shoe is placed into a furnace or fire until it is red hot. The farrier then holds the shoe on to the hoof wall for a few seconds. When he takes it away he can see whether it fits and make the necessary adjustments. This looks rather horrifying and smells dreadful, but it is quite painless because the wall of the hoof is virtually dead

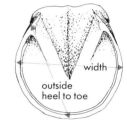

◄ **A traditional forge** where hot shoeing takes place on the premises.

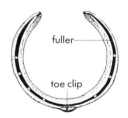

MEASURING THE FOOT
The farrier will measure the pony's foot for a new shoe but it's useful to know how to do it.

Pick up the foot and measure with a ruler from the outside heel edge to the toe; then across the widest part of the foot from the outside to the inside.

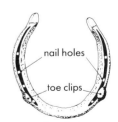

FRONT SHOE
A typical front shoe has one toe clip and seven nail holes. The groove (fullering) gives the shoe grip.

HIND SHOE
This has two toe clips on either side of the shoe toe.

When to shoe

There are several pointers that tell you when your horse needs shoeing:

● If the shoe has worn thin or become loose. The pony will be uncomfortable and a loose shoe could twist and make him lame.

● If the clenches (tips of the nails) have risen and stand out of the wall of the hoof. Instead of lying flat against the hoof, they stick out and could cut the pony.

● If the foot grows too long and out of shape. The hoof looks as though it has grown over the back of the shoe, but in fact what happens is that the foot draws the shoe forward as it grows longer.

● If the shoe has fallen off (been 'cast').

● If it is five weeks since the farrier last came. The shoes may still look fine, but you should have them taken off and the pony's feet pared (cut back) before the shoes are put back on. This is known as 'removes'.

▲ **The clenches have risen,** making the shoe loose and causing the hoof wall to crack.

The hot-shoeing method

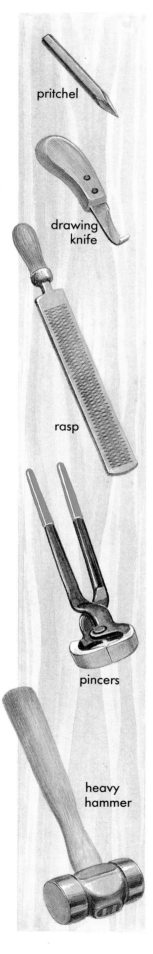

pritchel

drawing knife

rasp

pincers

heavy hammer

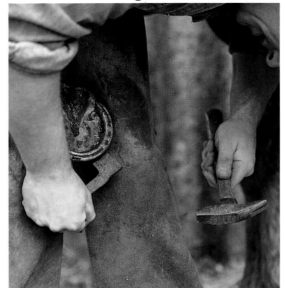

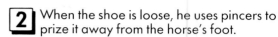
1 The farrier starts by taking off the old shoe. He uses the buffer and driving hammer to bring up the nail heads.

2 When the shoe is loose, he uses pincers to prize it away from the horse's foot.

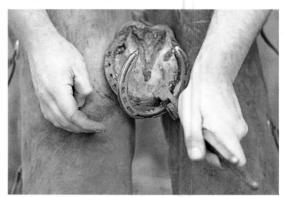

5 Meanwhile, the shoe heats up in the furnace (inset). The farrier shapes the shoe on the anvil, using the heavy hammer.

6 The shoe is held by a nail hole with the pritchel (shaped like a pencil) while it is tried on the foot. The farrier has the drawing knife in his other hand.

tissue, like our nails.

Once the farrier is satisfied that the shoe fits correctly, he submerges it in a bucket of cold water until it has cooled down. When he's prepared shoes for each foot, he nails them on, making sure that the nails only go into the hoof wall and not into the sensitive laminae.

The farrier turns the nail tips and twists them off, leaving enough to form a clench (a small 'hook', which helps to hold the shoe on). Finally, he rasps a small groove for the clench to lie in against the wall of the hoof.

Cold shoeing is when the farrier puts on a machine-made shoe: he may adjust the shoe beforehand or (to a limited extent) on the day.

The well-shod pony

It is most important that your pony is well shod. Look out for the following indicators.

☐ The shoe must fit the foot, not the other way round – the hoof wall should not be rasped away to meet the iron.

☐ The pony must be comfortable, with a shoe suitable for the work he has to do, neither too light or too heavy.

☐ The hoof wall should be trimmed to remove excess horn growth.

☐ The nails should appear at roughly the same height up the hoof. They should be the correct size so that the heads sit neatly in the holes of the shoe.

☐ There should be no daylight between the hoof and the shoe.

3 The farrier prepares the foot by trimming off the overgrown horn. He also tidies up the sole and frog by cutting away ragged bits.

4 He rasps the sole to make it level. At the same time, he can look at the condition and shape of the foot.

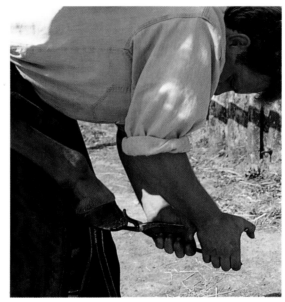

7 When the shoe is cool, the driving hammer is used to nail it on, starting at the toe. The right-sized nails must be chosen.

8 With pincers, the ends of the nails are drawn down to make clenches (hooks) and the shoe is tightened.

9 Finally, the clenches are rasped and embedded in the wall, and the rasp is used to smooth the outside of the wall where it meets the shoe. This helps stop the wall cracking.

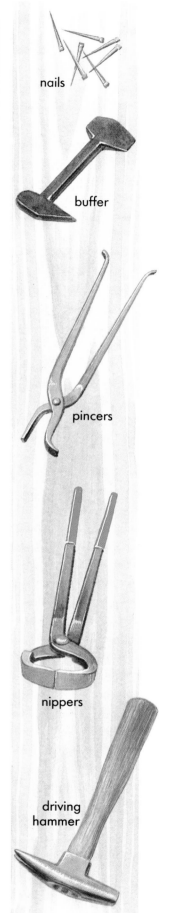

nails

buffer

pincers

nippers

driving hammer

Tail bandaging

Tail bandages have two purposes: they improve appearance by flattening the hair on the dock (top of the tail), and they protect the tail from rubbing when travelling.

Putting the bandage on

Tail bandages are made of stockinette or crêpe. Both these fabrics are stretchy, so dampen the hair before bandaging. (If you are bandaging for appearance's sake you have probably washed the tail first anyway.) Do not dampen the bandage in case it shrinks while on the tail and becomes too tight.

With bandage in hand, move behind the pony, putting a warning hand on his hindquarters to let him know where you are. Put the dock over your shoulder if the pony tries to clamp his tail down between his hindlegs.

Unroll the loose end of the bandage and leave a short strip to spare. Roll once round the top of the tail. Bring the spare end down over your turn and cover it with another roll to anchor the bandage. Carry on bandaging to two thirds of the way down the dock.

Once you reach the tapes, tie them in a bow on the outside (toward you). Tuck

▼ **Practise bandaging** the tail until you get the feel of just how tight to make it. The horse can enjoy a snooze in the sun while you work! Here the bandage is being used to improve appearance.

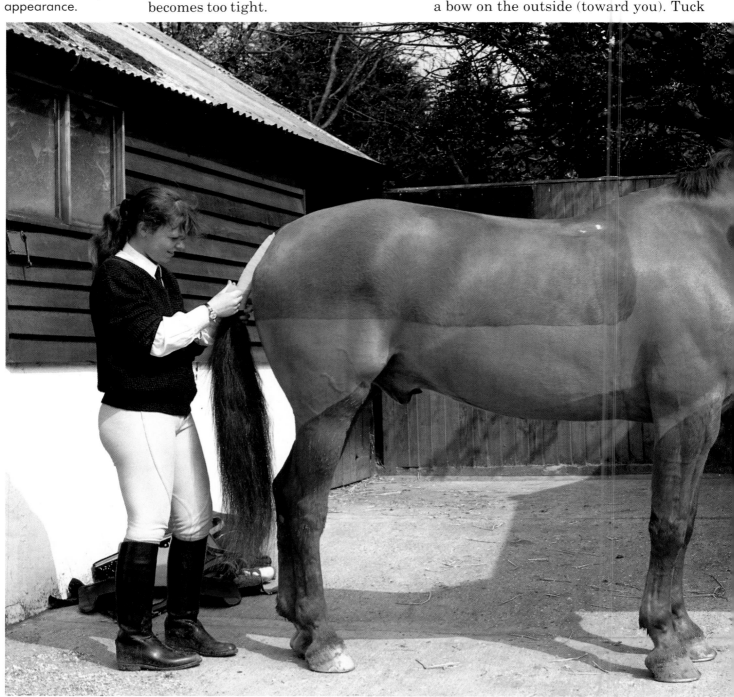

in the tapes neatly underneath the bandage. Bend the dock back into a comfortable, natural curve – the process of bandaging pulls it out of shape.

Of all the tack and clothing you put on a pony, bandages are probably the trickiest to do correctly. If they are too tight, the hair at the roots dies, falls out and regrows white. Wavy hair on the dock is a sign of a tail bandage that's been put on too tightly.

If it is too loose, however, the bandage can trail off and trip up the pony. Aim to bandage firmly but without cramping the tail.

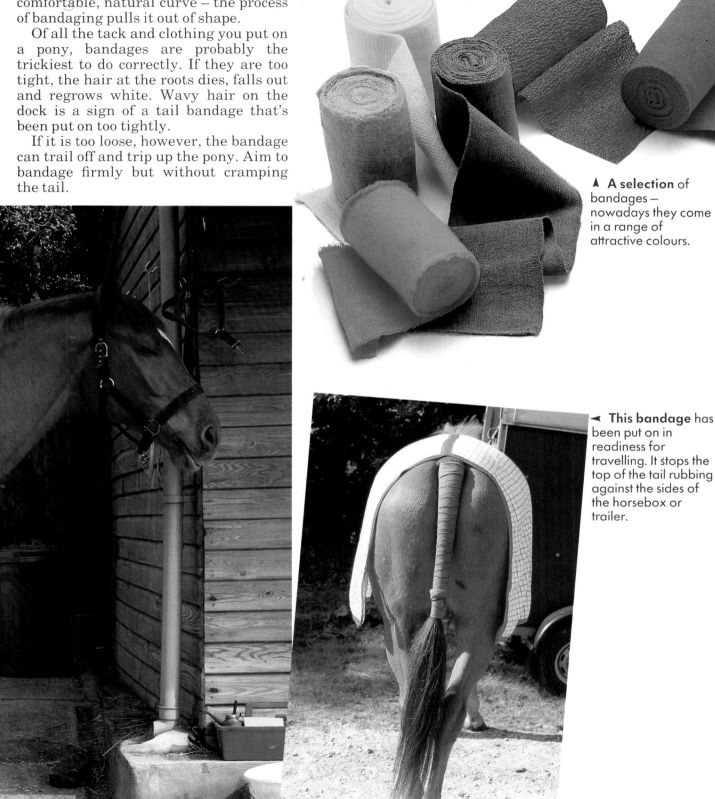

▲ **A selection** of bandages – nowadays they come in a range of attractive colours.

◄ **This bandage** has been put on in readiness for travelling. It stops the top of the tail rubbing against the sides of the horsebox or trailer.

How to put on a tail bandage

1 After dampening the top of the tail with a water brush, unroll the straight edge leaving about 15cm (6in) to spare.

2 Bandage once round under the tail, holding the spare edge out of the way. This is easier if you put the tail over your shoulder.

★ **MIX AND MATCH**

With the range of colours available now, you can give your pony a really smart appearance by matching his accessories.

If you have a nylon headcollar, use that as your base colour. Every time you get a new piece of equipment, choose the same colour. So, for instance, you could end up with a blue headcollar, blue tail and leg bandages, blue numnah and rug.

5 Roll back up again if you haven't yet reached the tapes at the end of the bandage. When you've used up the entire length, pull the tapes apart.

6 Wind the tapes around the bandage. Tie them on the outside (nearest to you) with a double bow so that the fastening doesn't come undone. Don't tie them *too* tightly or you could kill the hair at the roots.

3 Bring the flap down and secure it with another turn. This stage is crucial – if you work too loosely the bandage falls off.

4 Continue bandaging to two thirds of the way down the dock. Try to keep the bandage flat and the overlaps even.

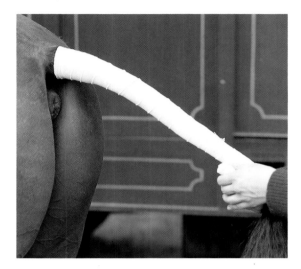

7 Tuck the tapes in for security and so there are no loose, untidy ends. Put your arm under the dock to bend the tail back into its smooth, natural curve. You now have a neat, well-fitting tail bandage.

Taking off the bandage

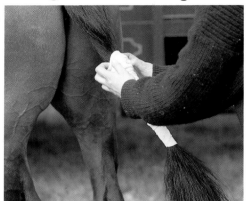

◄ **To remove**, grip around the top of the tail and simply slide the bandage off. Leave tail bandages on for a maximum of two hours or for the time the journey takes if travelling.

Rolling up the bandage

Once you have taken off the bandage, always roll it up. When you can, iron it first. But if you've just transported your pony to a show, that has to wait until you get home.

1 Hold the bandage at the tape end, sewn side up. Pull the tapes clear.

2 Wind the tapes around your fingers as if you are rolling up a ball of wool.

3 Fold them neatly across the triangular end of the bandage so the tapes form a 'core'.

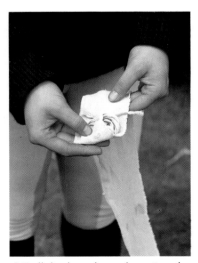

4 Roll the bandage, keeping the sewn side inward until you end with the straight edge outside.

Leg bandaging

Leg bandages can go on all four of the horse's legs. There are two types: stable bandages for warmth and drying off legs in cold weather and for protection when travelling; and exercise bandages to guard against knocks when riding.

Exercise bandages

Also called work bandages, these are usually made of stretchy fabric or knitted cotton stockinette. One end is straight and the other pointed, with tapes sewn on.

They go on over padding (gamgee tissue, special leg padding from a saddler or, not so good, plastic foam). The padding helps lessen any uneven pressure, as the bandage must be firm but not too tight.

Exercise bandages act as a buffer if the horse knocks his leg and, to some extent, prevent jarring. However, they do not support tendons. To do that, they would have to be put on around a joint, such as the fetlock, and restrict its movement to reduce strain on the tendons. But this would also hamper the free leg action needed during work.

So exercise bandages go from just below the hocks (on the hindlegs) or knees (on the forelegs) to just above the broad part of the fetlock. Some saddlers stock different lengths of bandage: pony, cob or full sizes.

Stable bandages

Stable (also described as 'travelling') bandages are longer and wider than exercise bandages. The easiest to use are of fine-knitted wool which moulds to the leg. They cushion the leg from knocks when travelling and keep stabled horses' legs warm and dry in winter.

Stable bandages go on just the same as exercise bandages but usually have Velcro fastenings rather than tapes. Instead of stopping at the fetlock, these bandages, plus their padding, go right over the fetlock and pastern to the heels and coronet (top of the hoof). Unfortunately, many are rather short and you may need to sew two together to make a good long bandage.

◄ **Stable bandages** (main picture) go right down over the fetlocks and pasterns and protect the legs when travelling. Exercise bandages (inset) go down to just above the fetlock and stop the legs jarring during work.

TRAVELLING PADS
Travelling pads are quick to put on if you haven't the time to leg bandage, but should *only* be used for travelling – not for exercise or in the stable.

They are usually made of plastic on the outside, and always padded on the inside. They fasten with strips of Velcro and are sometimes shaped with darts. The padding shields all four legs from knocks, but does not support the legs.

Starting to bandage

So that you get the feel of just how tight to work, it's best to practise on a drainpipe or young tree trunk before trying out bandaging on the pony.

You should be able to get your fingertip in a turn of the bandage and pull it away from the leg, but not too easily. Stable bandages should be slightly looser than exercise ones.

Cut the padding so it goes a little above and below the finished bandage and wrap it round the leg. You'll soon learn the knack of keeping it on while starting the bandage, and of keeping it smooth during bandaging. The padding stays put better if you damp the leg hair first.

Start with the near foreleg. Crouch down beside it. Never kneel because you can't get up quickly enough for safety should the pony play up at all.

Dressed for exercise

Hold the rolled bandage in your right hand with the loose straight end furthest from you opening to the left. Unroll about 20cm (8in) and place it diagonally across the leg, end uppermost, with the roll just below the knee.

Putting on a stable bandage

1 Cut the padding generously to come slightly above and below the bandage. Wrap it round the leg.

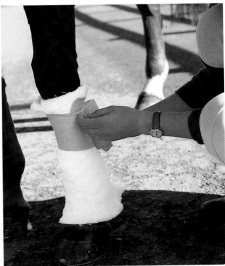

2 Keeping the padding smooth and secure, wind one roll of the bandage, leaving a flap at the end.

3 Fold the flap over the bandage and make another turn to cover the flap and anchor it.

➤ **Once you have completed** bandaging all four legs, the pony is ready for travel or for keeping warm in the stable. But because the bandages go right over the fetlock they restrict movement and cannot be used when exercising.

Most stable bandages now fasten with Velcro. Velcro has two advantages over tapes: it is quicker and easier to do up, and the pressure is even all the way round the leg. With tapes, it is all too easy to make pressure points where you tie the fastening.

Do one turn anti-clockwise right round the leg. Let the loose end drop down the outside of the leg and do another turn over it to anchor it. Keep rolling down to the fetlock covering half the bandage's width at each turn.

At the broadest part of the fetlock, turn upward and roll up to the knee. Roll firmly but do *not* stretch the material as it has a self-tightening effect anyway.

Finishing off

Try to finish with the pointed end toward the tail (so twigs don't catch in it if the pony brushes through undergrowth). Make sure the tapes aren't twisted, and tie them round the leg, one to the left and one to the right and back facing you again. Finish with a firm bow.

Tie the tapes *the same* tightness as the bandage itself, no tighter. You may want to cut the tapes if they are very long. Tuck the ends of the bow into a turn of the bandage so they don't get caught – and you've finished.

Always tie the tapes at the side of the leg and on the outside. If you tie them on the front bone or back tendons, you will create a lumpy pressure point, and on the inside the pony could kick the tapes undone.

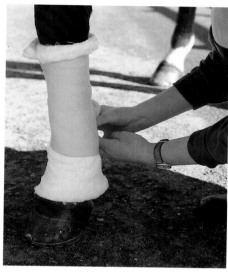

4 Roll down over the fetlock and pastern to the heel, overlapping about half the width every time.

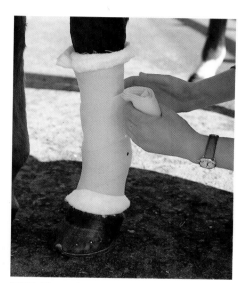

5 If you have any bandage to spare, roll back up, remembering to keep an even tension all the way.

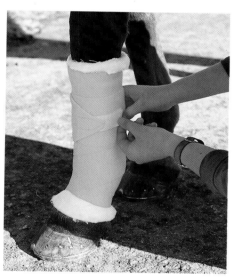

6 When you reach the Velcro, press the two strips together so that the bandage is held firmly in position.

Taking off a bandage

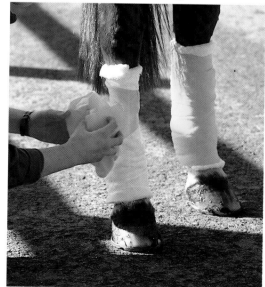

Peel the Velcro apart and unravel the bandage, passing it from hand to hand.

Run your hand briskly down the leg several times to restore circulation.

Clipping your pony

All horses grow a new coat for the winter, although moorland-type ponies grow denser, more furry coats, and cob-types grow longer, shaggier coats than Thoroughbreds, Arabs and other fine breeds. So, in early autumn, you must decide how you plan to keep and use your pony through the winter, and whether or not to have him clipped.

An unclipped pony

Unclipped, with his natural fur coat on, your pony should be able to live out, day and night all winter through – although fine-bred and very old ponies may need a New Zealand rug for extra protection.

But make sure your pony has as much good quality hay, fresh every day, as he will eat. He may also need concentrates – such as pony cubes – to keep him plump, cheerful and lively throughout the winter. A pony who is not getting enough food to keep his system stoked up quickly loses condition, particularly toward the end of winter. So keep checking, and adjust his feed as necessary; a thick coat may well be hiding a thin pony.

An unclipped pony looks shaggy rather than smart. You should not attempt to groom him deep down with a body brush. He needs the grease in his coat as protection against cold and wet.

Provided you feed him properly, he will be well up to quiet riding. If you ride him regularly, you can get him fit enough for a short day out – to compete in the odd class or at an indoor show. But do not expect too much.

Winter fitness

You cannot get an unclipped pony really fit. With his heavy coat on, fast work ►

▼ **Shaggy ponies** quickly become hot and exhausted if they are exercised too much without being clipped.

A trace clip like this is a good compromise for a hardy pony; you can get him fit enough for competitions and jumping while still wintering him in a field.

Types of clip

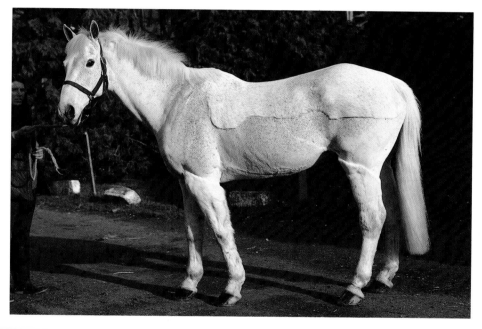

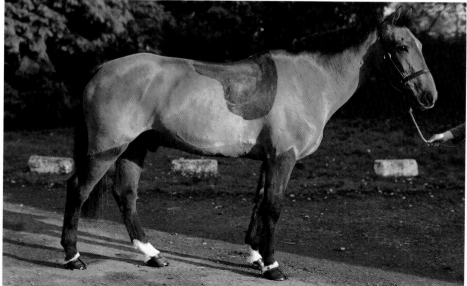

◄ **The trace clip** follows the line of the harness horse's traces — halfway up the pony's sides. This useful, practical style dates from the days of horse-drawn transport. The line of the clip continues up the pony's neck. Traditionally, his head is clipped, but modern variations may leave the head wholly unclipped. Alternatively, long, woolly hair under a pony's jaw may be clipped while the face is left alone.

This is a good clip for an owner who has stabling and wants the pony fit, but cannot exercise him every day. Unless he is very delicate, a trace-clipped pony, made fit in autumn, can be turned out in a New Zealand rug to exercise himself on most winter days when he cannot be ridden.

➤ **Blanket clip:** The horse's head, neck and body are clipped, except for the area an exercise sheet would cover — the back, loins and quarters. The leg hair is left on.

Gullet clip: If you only have a field to keep your pony in but he becomes hot, wet and unhappy whenever you ride him, a gullet clip may be the answer. Hair is removed on the pony's belly and between his forelegs. The clipped portion tapers upward in a V-shape to a point halfway up the underside of the pony's neck.

A gullet-clipped pony does not look as if he is clipped, but he stands work better, without losing the benefit of his winter coat. Use your common sense, however, about the work you give him. No pony in winter — indeed no pony at all — should be pulled out of his field, unfit, for hours of galloping.

◄ **Hunter clip:** The horse's head, neck and body (except for a saddle patch) are clipped. The hair is left on the legs for protection against cold and thorns.

Full clip: The coat is taken off from nose to toe. This is also known as 'clipping a horse right out'.

Either a full or a hunter clip means you must keep your horse stabled for the whole of the winter. You must decide whether you have the time and facilities to keep your pony in this way: daily mucking out and grooming, giving hay, water and feed at least twice a day and exercising the horse for at least an hour, six days out of seven.

RUG CARE

Whatever rug you choose for a clipped pony, it must be correctly fitted and put on. It should also be removed and replaced at least once a day — left in place too long, rugs chafe and rub. See page 123 for step-by-step photographs of rugging up.

★ CLIPPING WITH EASE

Properly done, with good sharp blades, clipping does not hurt the pony at all. Most soon grow used to the noise of the clippers.

Clipping is done against the lie of the coat — from back to front. So there is time for the pony to settle before the tricky parts like the head are reached.

makes a pony sweat heavily, just as a person would if he went for a cross-country run wearing several sweaters and a thick jacket.

Your pony becomes wet, hot, tired and distressed if you ride him hard when he is not clipped. And, after riding, he may become chilled before you can get him dry. He will lose weight and condition. If you want your pony fully fit for winter work, you need to have him clipped.

The clipped pony

Clipping involves shaving off a horse's coat, over all or part of his body. It is usually done with electrically operated clippers and is not a job for the inexperienced pony-keeper to tackle.

A local stable-owner may provide a clipping service. Otherwise, the nearest Pony Club branch or riding club should be able to advise you.

The clipped pony needs stable cloth-

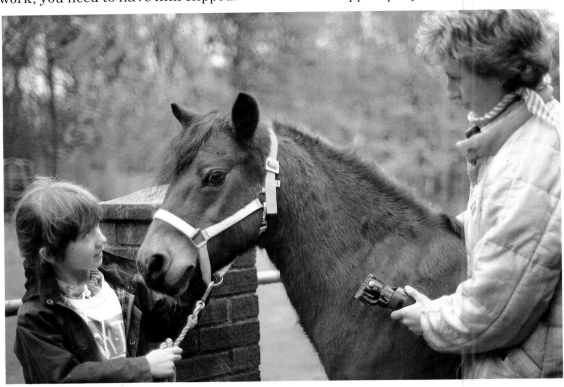

▲ **Soothing the pony:** Stand by the pony's head and talk to him so you keep him occupied while he is clipped. At the same time you can watch the expert at work.

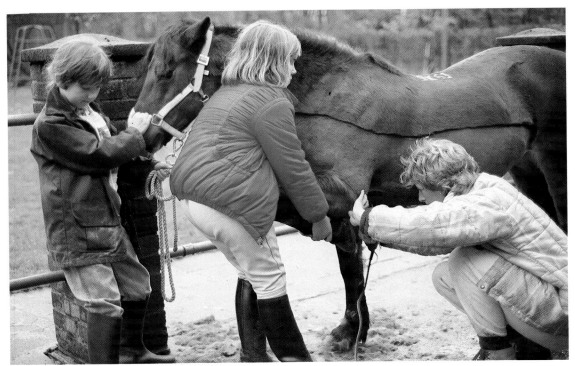

◄ **You can help** by stretching the front leg forward when the pony's girth and elbows are clipped. This helps to avoid nipping any loose folds of skin.

ing to wear in place of his natural coat when he is not working. Modern stable rugs – like duvets, with built-in surcingles and/or leg straps – give warmth without weight, and need no roller.

When to clip

A pony's winter coat starts growing in early autumn. He should be clipped for the first time in mid-autumn, before his coat becomes too long. The coat goes on growing afterwards, so he'll need a second clip early in winter.

By mid to late winter, the summer coat starts to grow. If you want to do competition work in spring, clip again in mid-winter. But if you want to turn the pony out again when the weather is warm enough, avoid a third clip. Just remove the long 'cat' hairs that develop along the line of the neck and hindquarters to smarten him up.

Getting your pony ready

Before clipping, your pony should be stabled and ridden regularly for a week or so if possible. After riding, sponge him down with warm water to remove grease that may clog the clippers – but dry him well so he doesn't get chilled.

The pony should be clean and dry on the day. And remember to wear something that horse hair does not stick to! Handle him in a calm, matter-of-fact way so he is quite happy to be clipped. In any case, clipping seldom takes more than an hour.

You can ride your pony home after he is clipped, but bring an exercise sheet to save him from catching cold. Rug him up if you are boxing him home – never leave a clipped pony standing in the stable without clothing. Use the body brush rather than the dandy brush to groom him once he is clipped.

▼ **Chaser clip before and after:** This is a high-cut, modern variation of the trace clip. The chaser clip is so called because it can be used on steeplechasers to keep their backs warm.

It is an excellent choice for ponies who are stabled but sometimes turned out during the day.

Trimming your pony

Unless your pony is a native breed, trimming makes him look much smarter, particularly for showing.

Before you start

Before you start trimming, groom the pony to remove any excess dirt and mud. There's no need to wash him first, but it is a good idea to give him a thorough bath with horse shampoo afterwards to remove any loose hair. Choose a warm day so he doesn't get chilled.

For trimming you need round-ended scissors and a mane comb. If you have them, electric or hand clippers are also useful.

The legs

The feather, which grows at the back of the fetlock joints, can be cut back with either clippers or scissors. When using clippers make sure that you don't go too close, as you do not want a skinned look.

Start with the forelegs. Remove the long hair from below the pony's knee right down to his pastern. When using scissors, lift the hair with the mane comb and pull it taut so you cut evenly and don't leave the pony looking 'chewed' – work as if you are cutting a person's hair. Either cut downward or upward but not across, so you get a smooth finish.

When trimming the hindlegs be wary of your pony kicking. Crouch down – don't kneel – beside (not behind) the leg.

You can also cut carefully round the top of the foot with the scissors to remove long hairs growing over the hoof wall.

Some experts believe that you should not trim your pony's feather in winter. They feel that feather helps to keep the pony's legs warm and protect them from mud fever or cracked heels. However, if you don't trim the legs it is difficult to spot the first signs of trouble. If you are not sure about winter trimming, ask ➤

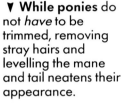

▼ **While ponies** do not *have* to be trimmed, removing stray hairs and levelling the mane and tail neatens their appearance.

Trimming checklist – what to remember

● DO tie the pony up with a quick-release knot in case the clippers scare him.

● DO groom the pony thoroughly before you start.

● DO choose a warm day if you're going to wash the pony afterwards, otherwise he might get chilled.

● DO use round-ended scissors to reduce the risk of accidental cuts.

● DO make sure that your clippers are in perfect working order.

● DON'T kneel down when you trim the hindlegs.

● DON'T cut the eyelashes.

● DON'T let any hair fall into the ear.

● DON'T use electric clippers on the head of a nervous pony.

● DON'T cut the feather straight across.

▲ **Tie the pony up** with a quick-release knot and give him a thorough groom before you start trimming.

The legs and feet

1 Lift the feather away from the leg with the mane comb. Cut the hair jutting through the teeth of the comb on a *slope*, not across, or you will end up with a series of jagged layers.

2 Cut evenly around the coronet so that the hair meets the hoof wall in a clear line.

3 Snip off any stray hairs growing down the back of the leg. Hold the tail out of the way so you can see what you're doing.

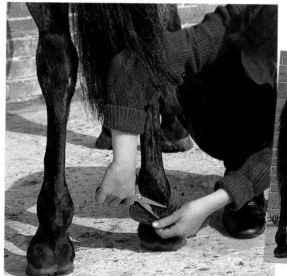

4 Trim the hindleg feather as you did the forelegs. Crouch close to the pony's side just in case he kicks out.

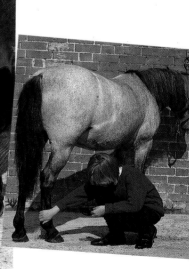

▲ **Check** you haven't missed out any hairs. All four legs should feel smooth and even.

the advice of your vet or instructor – someone who knows your pony.

The head and ears

To make your pony's head look well-defined, you can remove the facial whiskers – which it is thought horses do not need for feeling as, say, a cat does. Snip off the long hairs around his chin and muzzle, between his cheek bones and down the underside of his head. *Never* cut the eyelashes.

The whiskery hair that comes out of the ears and the excess hair growing round the edge of the ears can also be trimmed to neaten the pony's head. Work extremely carefully as *no* hair must drop into the ear – this causes considerable discomfort and distress.

To trim the outer edge, hold the ear so

Trimming the ears and muzzle

1 Hold the pony's head still with your free hand. Very carefully, snip off the whiskers round the muzzle and chin.

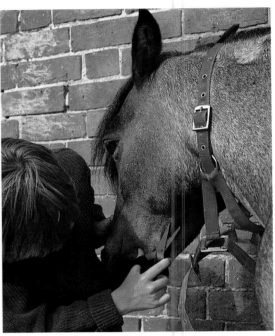

2 Undo the headcollar and tie it round the pony's neck. As long as he is quiet, trim the hair under his head and on his cheek bones.

3 Gently press the sides of the ear together so no hair can fall in. Cut the hairs sticking out along the edges.

4 With the comb, part the mane in a straight line about 5cm (2in) behind the ears. Cut a path for the headpiece to lie on.

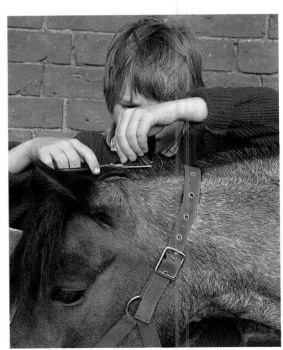

TRIMMING THE TAIL

Most pony's tails are too long. When the tail is 'carried' (when the pony is moving and holding his tail up), a practical length is to have the end in line with the hocks.

It's much easier to work out the length if a friend lifts the tail up to the position it is in when carried. Cut it across with clippers or scissors.

The pony's tail should be pulled, unless you plait it, so that it lies neatly against the quarters. For more information on trimming, pulling and plaiting the tail, see pages 158–161.

To stop the mane becoming long and straggly it should also be pulled. This is described on page 163.

that the sides are together and there are no gaps for hair to drop in. Use either scissors or clippers – although some horses won't tolerate electric clippers near their heads – and cut along the edges, taking great care not to cut the ear itself.

The pony looks neater if you trim away the mane where the headpiece of the bridle lies, just behind the ears. Use the mane comb to separate a straight line of about 3-5cm (1½-2in) from the rest of the mane, and cut it off at the base with the scissors.

You can also trim the mane over the withers. But if the pony often wears a rug you may prefer to leave the mane intact so that it can help protect the withers from getting rubbed by the rug and becoming sore.

When *not* to trim

Certain breeds, such as Arabs, Welsh ponies and Fells, always keep their manes and tails long. The Mountain and Moorland breeds do not have their feather trimmed.

Heavy horses like Shires and Clydesdales have beautiful long manes and feather, but their tails are trimmed in a special style if they are going to be shown.

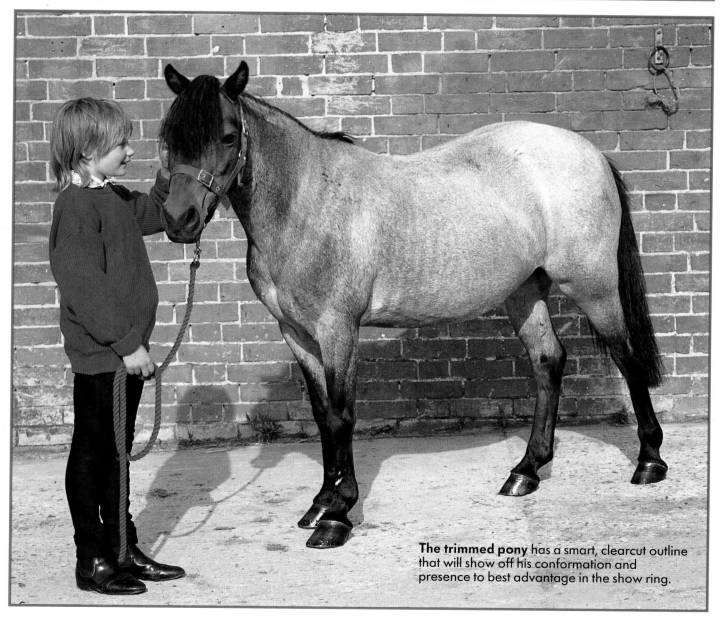

The trimmed pony has a smart, clearcut outline that will show off his conformation and presence to best advantage in the show ring.

Plaiting the tail

Plaiting your pony's tail smartens up his appearance when you go to a show or competition. It's easy to do once you've got the knack. Alternatively, you can pull (layer) the tail.

Getting the pony ready

Before you start plaiting, the tail needs to be well-brushed, clean and damp. Start by washing it. Sometimes a tail that's just been washed is so 'squeaky' clean it's difficult to handle. In this case, wash the tail a week before the day and dampen it just before plaiting.

Always use a specially prepared horse shampoo or pure soap, never a detergent which can irritate the skin. You'll also need a bucket with warm soapy water and one with warm rinsing water, two sponges and an old towel.

Plaiting equipment

The tail has to be tangle-free for plaiting, so have handy a water brush and tail comb (which is exactly the same as a mane comb).

Once you've plaited the tail you sew it up. For this you need strong thread, a needle, and scissors to cut the thread. The thread should be about 60cm (2ft) long, doubled and knotted at the end. Choose the same colour as the pony's tail so it doesn't show. But so *you* don't lose sight of it while you are plaiting, carefully pin the needle on to your jacket or jersey.

◄ **The confidence** you feel from knowing your pony is groomed and plaited to perfection means you're already halfway to gaining first prize!

Washing the tail

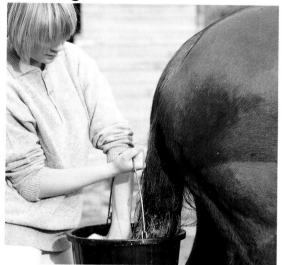

1 If your pony is quiet, you can stand behind him. Otherwise, work from beside his quarters. Put the tail in the soapy water.

2 Put the bucket on the ground to wash the top of the tail. Run your hands down the tail, squeezing it to get rid of excess water.

★ **RINSING AND DRYING**
You may need several buckets of rinsing water, as you must get all the soap out of the tail.

For a placid pony, you can dry the tail by swinging it round like a helicopter propeller. If your pony doesn't like you doing this, use an old towel to rub it so that it is just damp.

Brush the hair with the water brush, and the tail is ready to plait.

3 Rub the tail either between your hands or with the sponge. Keep dipping the tail into the soapy water until it feels clean.

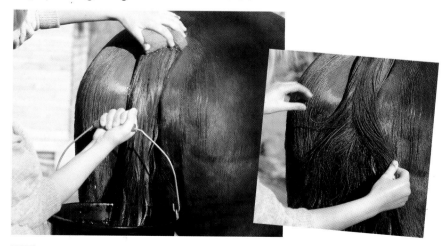

4 Switch to the bucket of warm rinsing water. With the tail in the bucket, rinse the top down using your clean sponge.

▲ Pull the hairs apart to check you've removed all the soap.

How to plait

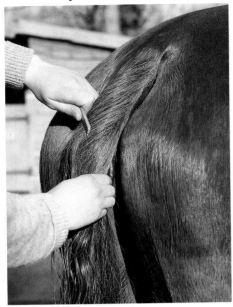  

1 Thoroughly comb the hair with the tail comb, particularly the sides, which you will join in to the top of the plait. Work down to about 10-15cm (4-6in) from the end of the dock.

2 Take a small amount of long tail hair from either side edge and the same amount from the middle and start to plait. Every second or third plait, join in more hair from the side edges.

3 Plait as tightly as possible and continue down the tail to about 10-15cm (4-6in) from the end of the dock. Go on plaiting without taking hair from the sides.

Pulling the tail

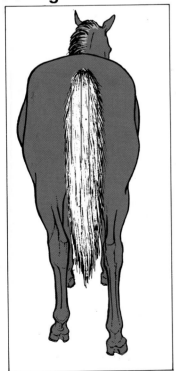 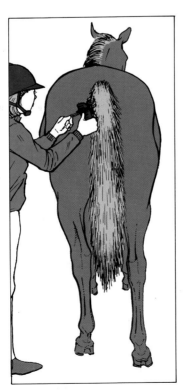 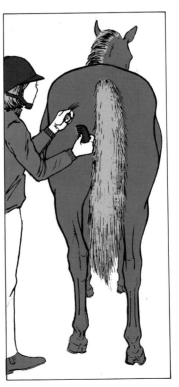 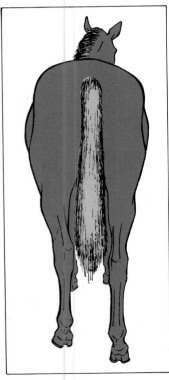

1 Imagine four or five lines running from the top of the tail down to about 7.5cm (3in) below the point of the buttock. These help you pull the tail evenly.

2 Take a few hairs at a time from each section between the lines: one on either side of the tail and several in the centre. Wrap the hairs round the tail comb.

3 Pull quickly downward so that the hair comes away with the comb. Only do a little at a time, and don't carry on too long or the pony will become bored, restive and sore.

4 The tail should be levelly pulled, and sit neatly against the hindquarters. It may take several days to complete. Wash the tail thoroughly and bandage it afterwards.

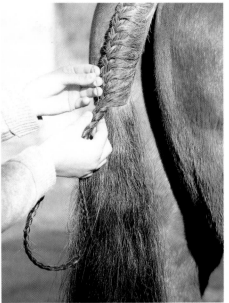

4 When you reach the end of the hair, secure the plait with the needle and thread. Sew through the end, and wrap the thread round it a few times. Sew through the plait again.

5 Fold the long plait up in one big loop. Secure it to the underside of the base of the French plait by sewing through the middle of both plaits. Be as neat as possible.

6 Fasten off by winding the thread round the loop to stop it coming undone. Cut off any thread left over with the scissors. The thread should hardly be visible.

The techniques

When you plait the tail you use two techniques. Both methods use three strands of hair to make the plait. But in the first (called French plaiting) you join in more hair from the sides as you go along. The plait stands out from the tail if you bring the side hair in from *underneath*; if you add the hair to the *top* of your strands, the plait appears flat.

The second method is just a normal plait without any hair taken from the sides. Combine both techniques – with a French plait to the bottom of the dock, and a normal plait to the end of the tail hair.

To hold the plait in place, dampen the tail again – it will probably have dried out – and put on a tail bandage. Remember when removing the tail bandage to unroll it and not pull it off – or all your hard work could be wasted.

If your pony's tail is not thick enough to plait and you want it to look smart, you can pull it. This means pulling hair out of the upper part of the tail so the hair is thinned out – similar to layering your own hair.

Do not be tempted to use clippers or thinning scissors – when the hair grows again the top of the tail could resemble a scrubbing brush.

Trimming the tail

The length of the tail should be about 10-15cm (4-6in) below the point of hock. You can either leave the tail uneven at the bottom (a 'swish' tail), or cut it straight across with the scissors or clippers (a 'bang' tail).

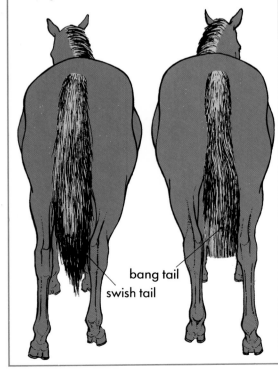

bang tail
swish tail

▲ **It's smartest** to sew the halves of the loop together all the way down so the plait lies flat. When you've finished sewing, the plait should be secure, with no sign of the end of the tail.

Plaiting the mane

▼ **Practice makes perfect:** It takes an expert touch to produce a turn-out like this champion Polish Arab stallion at the Canberra Show in Australia.

When you go to a show, dressage competition or any special occasion, it adds to your confidence to know your pony is well turned out. Plaiting the mane neatly is an art that improves with practice, so you may need a few trial runs at home first.

Pulling the mane

It is virtually impossible to plait a mane or forelock in the traditional way if it is very long and thick. Before attempting to plait, you need to pull both the mane and forelock to about 10cm (4in) in length.

As the mane should always hang down to the right, stand on the off side of the pony. Start by brushing the pony's mane with the water brush. When it is tangle-free, take the mane comb and thoroughly comb the hair.

It is easiest to work down the neck from behind the pony's ears to his withers. Pull out the longest pieces of hair first. To get the correct amount of hair, hold a small amount in your left hand. With your mane comb in your right hand, push the comb up the hair toward the pony's crest, so that you are left with a few strands of hair in your hand.

Repeat the action, then wrap the remaining strands round the mane comb and pull downward firmly, or just tweak the hair out with your left hand. Pull the forelock in the same fashion as the mane.

If you are left-handed, reverse the instructions.

Getting ready

The mane should be clean before you plait it, so wash it with mild shampoo. Do this a few days before, as immediately after the wash the hair is more difficult to handle. Be careful not to get any water in the pony's ears or eyes.

Gather together the equipment you'll

How to pull the mane

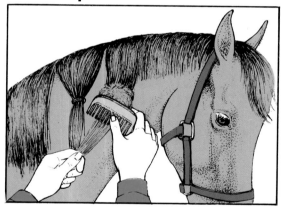

1 Take a small section of hair, hold it taut and push the mane comb up it.

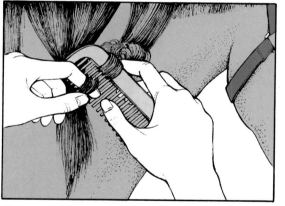

2 Repeat, so you are left with fewer strands, and wrap the hair that's left round the comb.

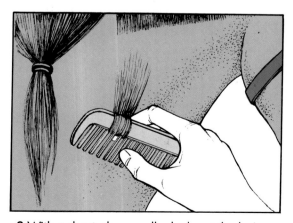

3 With a short, sharp pull, pluck out the hair.

► The mane should be an even 10cm (4in) in length.

❗ KEEP IT
● SHORT

It is easiest to pull the pony's mane after exercise when the pony is warm and his pores are open. Only pull a little at a time, or the pony becomes bored and sore and you get blisters.

Avoid the temptation to give up using your mane comb for a pair of thinning or ordinary scissors — your pony's mane will look terrible and be extremely difficult to plait.

HOW MANY PLAITS?

Use the mane comb to work out how many plaits you need. Hold it at the top of the mane, and turn it over and over down to the withers, counting one plait for each comb's width.

You should plait an odd number so, if you end on an even number, do one more or less. Flatter your pony's shape by making it one less if his neck is long and thin; one more if it is a bit stubby.

It is fashionable in some sports, notably show jumping, to do a large number of much smaller plaits.

★ THE FORELOCK

You plait the forelock slightly differently from the mane. Start off in the same way as you plait the tail — incorporating hair from either side as well as from the middle. This means you can pick up wispy pieces of hair that grow round the poll.

Work down until you come to the main part of the forelock, then plait as for the mane.

need: water brush, mane comb, plaiting or strong button thread or elastic bands (the colour of the mane and forelock), a bodkin-type needle, scissors and water. Cut about 150cm (5ft) of thread and thread the needle. Double it and tie a knot at the end. Pin the needle into your jacket so you don't lose it.

Use the mane comb to calculate how many plaits you are going to do. Hold the comb in your right hand, and place it at the top of the mane behind the ears. Turn the comb lengthwise down the crest, keeping a count of the number of times you do it as this is how many plaits you need. It is traditional to make an odd number of plaits, so you may need to take slightly less or more than a mane comb's width per plait.

How to plait

Beginning at the top of the pony's neck behind the ears, gather your comb's width of mane. Divide the hair into three equal parts and plait as you would do for a person. Make it as tight as

How to plait with needle and thread

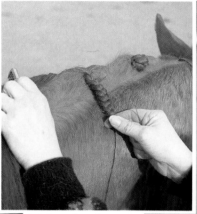

1 Plait as far down as you can. Sew up through the end of the plait several times, passing the needle to right and left alternately.

2 Fold the plait up and sew through the centre of it close to the crest.

3 Roll the plait up again so it is one quarter of its original length. Sew up through it until the plait is securely fixed, passing the needle from right to left as before. Fasten off on the underside.

If you are using elastic bands instead of thread, twist them round the plait at each stage. The band must be tightly stretched at the end to keep the plait secure.

Plaiting equipment: Shampoo the mane about a week before. You need special horse shampoo, a sponge and water for washing, and plenty of clean water for rinsing. Dry the mane with a towel.

Before you plait, damp down the mane and brush it on to the off side and also comb it. To fasten the plaits, use a blunt needle and thread, or elastic bands.

warm soapy water

warm rinsing water

rubber bands

sponge

horse shampoo

needle and plaiting thread

mane comb

towel

water brush

possible without hurting the pony. Plait close to the neck, not out toward yourself, and go down as far as you can.

Take your needle and thread and sew through the end of the plait, wrap the thread round the hair and sew through it again to stop it unravelling. Fold the plait under so your knot can't be seen. Bring the needle up through the middle of the plait so it comes out on the top side. Fold the plait again and sew through it once more, so you have quartered the length of the plait.

Fasten it securely as if you are sewing on a button: pull the thread round one side of the plait and up the middle, then round the other side and up the middle, and so on. Finish with the needle facing down and cut off the remaining thread.

Continue until you have plaited all the mane. The plaits should lie as tight as possible to the neck and stay firm even if you tug them.

Instead of using a needle and thread you can use elastic bands. This is quick but the plaits may come undone.

UNRULY MANES

Some ponies' manes are so unruly that they won't stay on one side of the neck, let alone on the off side where they are meant to be!

Try dampening the mane well and plaiting it on the off side, but without rolling the plaits up. Leave them in for a couple of days.

When you unplait the mane it should stay on one side, even if it is a bit wavy. Keep brushing it regularly and dampening it with your water brush.

◄ **A well-plaited mane** creates a good impression with the judges.

An alternative – high plaits

▲ **Hold the hair upward** as you plait, secure the end as normal, then thread the plait through the hair near the roots.

▲ **Coil the plait** round the loop, and secure with elastic bands or thread. These plaits sit on top of the crest and give more height.

The finishing touches

If you are showing your pony, his presentation is as important as his manners and action. A smartly turned-out pony 'takes the judge's eye' and gives you a better chance of winning.

The day before

Wash and shampoo the pony the day before the show, particularly if he spends time in a field. Use a horse shampoo or mild soap, never a detergent.

Check that the chestnuts and ergots are not protruding too much. If they are, gently pick them back with your fingers. Sometimes the ergots need cutting back. If you are worried about doing this, your farrier will help and can do it with his pincers.

Clean the tack thoroughly. If you have a coloured browband, you can put

that on for show pony classes, but not for show hunter pony or working pony classes. Try to use a girth that is a similar colour to your pony: a white girth on a dark bay, black or chestnut spoils his outline.

In the morning

On the morning of the show, groom your pony thoroughly. Plait his mane, unless you are going in for a breed class that

has specific requirements for presentation. In general, show ponies have pulled, not plaited, tails.

When you dampen the mane and forelock, put a little baby oil in the water. This makes the hair shine and helps to keep in any unruly strands.

Wash and dry round your pony's eyes, nose, muzzle and dock – in that order – and put baby oil gently on these and on the chestnuts. Baby oil defines the head

▼ **When the time comes** to line up for the judge's inspection, the most impressive pony will be correctly presented and in the peak of health.

Putting on quarter marks

1 Damp the quarters and place the stencil on top. It's easier to stop it shifting if a friend helps to hold it firmly in position.

2 When you have brushed the hair downward, carefully lift off the stencil, taking care not to rub the marks as you do so.

3 To keep the diamond pattern of marks in perfect formation, spray them with hair spray and don't touch them!

and makes it look prettier. You can use Vaseline or petroleum jelly instead of baby oil, but they sometimes become lumpy and don't give such a smooth finish.

If the pony has white socks, you can rub saddler's chalk on them to make them look even whiter.

Wipe the coat with the stable rubber, putting on coat polish (show gloss) if you have some. This makes the coat glow and keeps it free of dust.

The pony's feet should be smart, well-shod and perfectly clean. Put hoof oil on the underside of the hoof and on the outside. Be careful not to get any on his coronet band or hair.

Decorative patterns

When you have arrived at the show and taken your pony out of the box, go over the morning's finishing touches again.

You can now add quarter markings (a 'draught board' pattern of squares on the hindquarters) and shark's teeth (zigzags lower down the quarters), depending on what class you are entering the pony for.

For riding pony, best pony, leading-rein pony, hacks and riding horse classes, you can use both types of decoration. In show hunter pony and working pony classes just apply shark's teeth and maybe large blocks high up on the hindquarters.

Quarter markings

You can put quarter marks on with a comb or with a stencil. Practise at home until your work is perfect.

⭐ **WHITENING THE TAIL**
If your pony has a white tail, you may find the hairs at the end tend to go yellow. To make them gleaming white, try putting household fabric conditioner in the rinsing water when you wash the tail.

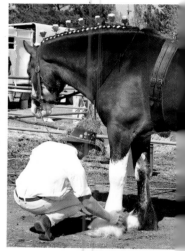

▲ **Rubbing chalk** on socks and feather — after washing them — makes them look as white as snow. You can buy chalk from a saddler.

Making quarter markings with a comb

Damp the coat and comb downward in alternate squares, starting each at the corner of the one above. The squares should all be the same size, and placed in the shape of a triangle pointing up or down.

In the comb method, buy a cheap plastic comb and break it to the size of square you want – the smaller the pony, the smaller the squares. Moisten the coat, and comb downward to make one square. From its bottom-left corner, comb downward again to make another square, then do the same from its bottom-right corner, and so on. Work in reverse if you prefer the point of the triangle facing down.

You can buy stencils with various sizes and styles of quarter marks. Damp the hair on the quarters with a flannel. Place the stencil on the quarter and brush the hair that shows through in a downward path. Remove the stencil.

To keep the quarter marks neat, spray them with hair spray. If your pony doesn't like the noise, use hair gel. In this case, damp the hair, put on the gel and smooth the hair in the correct direction *before* making the pattern.

Shark's teeth

Shark's teeth go on your pony's flanks and are made with a damp body brush. Stand behind the pony and brush triangles of hair toward you, against the grain. Work down to the thigh area, leaving intersecting diagonals of hair brushed with the grain, so you end with several 'teeth'. Use hair gel or spray as for quarter markings.

Remember that it is no use making these patterns unless your pony is fit and healthy with a naturally shiny coat.

Arab plaiting

An alternative to normal plaits is Arab plaiting, used on Arabs and on ponies with long manes such as palominos.

Brush the hair flat. Starting at the poll, divide the first mane comb's width of hair into three. Plait as normal, but add in a new strand from the left after every section of the plait. Make sure you keep the hair tight. When you reach the withers, sew up with thread.

◄ **Shark's teeth** and quarter markings are not merely a decoration: they improve the look and outline of the horse's quarters.

◄ **Quarter markings** complete the turn-out of a show pony that is glowing from health and thorough grooming.

The annual check up

You should always consult a vet if your pony becomes ill or lame. But you also need to call the vet in for routine procedures that keep the horse healthy and *prevent* disease.

A yearly visit

Your horse needs to be vaccinated against serious diseases such as tetanus and flu. He has booster vaccinations each year. The vet has to come to give your pony his injection, so it's a good time to make sure the horse is in tip-top shape all over.

The vet examines the pony's teeth thoroughly. He also studies the feet and skin to make sure there are no lumps or bumps or other problems.

An annual check up gives someone else – who hasn't seen the pony for a while – the chance to have a good look at him. Sometimes it's easier for another person to notice signs of, for example, stiffness or loss of condition, than for the person who sees the animal every day.

◄ **The vet feels the pony's legs** for any heat, lumps or swellings that may indicate splints or tendon trouble.

Making a note

A yearly visit is also the ideal time to ask the vet's advice on any aspects of your pony's health that are worrying you. These might include his body condition, feed, worming programme, the state of his feet or any shoeing problems. Similarly, if you have found any specific trouble areas, such as a skin growth or irritation, now is the time to ask the vet about it.

Sometimes you only remember what you wanted to ask just after the vet has driven away! So it is a sensible precaution to make a list of questions on a piece of paper beforehand. Then nothing gets forgotten.

Before the check up

Any time of year is suitable for the check up. However, you shouldn't work your pony hard for four or five days after a vaccination, in case he has side effects such as a stiff neck.

There are no specific preparations to make before the vet arrives. However, although he will be happy to spend time checking over the horse and answering your questions – he will not be happy to waste time waiting around while you

VACCINATION CERTIFICATES
Many authorities who organize equestrian events have made flu vaccinations compulsory for all horses entering their events. You need a vaccination certificate, on which the horse is identified and the date when boosters have been given is recorded.

Boosters given at the wrong interval can not only make the horse ineligible to compete, but could also prove expensive – as the vaccination programme may have to be started all over again.

◄ **Combined flu and tetanus vaccines** are available. Giving your horse a dose against both diseases forms the most essential part of the annual check up.

catch the pony, or to examine a horse that's covered in mud.

Catch a grass-kept pony an hour or so before the appointment. Give him a thorough grooming and pick out his feet. While you do so, study his skin, feet and legs yourself – then you can ask the vet about them if need be.

It's tricky to examine a horse's mouth if he has recently been eating. Keep him away from grass and hay, and give him his feed, at least an hour beforehand.

Tetanus vaccination

This is a major part of the annual check up. Vaccination – against the serious disease tetanus particularly – is one of the most important contributions you can make toward keeping your pony healthy.

Horses can easily pick up tetanus when wounds become contaminated with the tetanus organism which lives in the soil. Horses are particularly at risk because this organism sometimes lives inside their bowels. If the bowel wall becomes damaged in any way, the organism within the gut could enter the horse's body and cause tetanus.

The horse should be permanently vaccinated against tetanus. This means two initial injections of tetanus vaccine a month apart, and a booster one year later. Afterwards, the pony needs a booster at least every two to three years.

A pony that's not permanently vaccinated needs an injection of tetanus anti-toxin *every* time he receives a cut or a puncture wound (such as when a shoe nail from a loose shoe punctures the foot). The tetanus antitoxin works immediately, but its protection *only* lasts for three to four weeks.

Equine flu

This is another nasty disease which spreads rapidly from horse to horse in epidemics. It can also give the pony a nasty cough which lasts for several months.

The horse needs two primary vaccinations 21 days to 92 days apart, and a booster six months later. Afterwards, boosters must be given regularly every year.

The teeth

The second most important annual task is to check your pony's teeth. Ideally, the horse's upper and lower cheek teeth

▲ **The vet** listens to the pony's heart beat with a stethoscope.

► **He studies the eyes** to make sure there are no cataracts or other disorders that affect the pony's sight.

▼ **He may do a 'spavin test':** He holds the leg up high and then watches the pony being trotted away. Any stiffness or lameness shows up immediately.

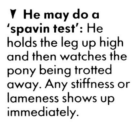

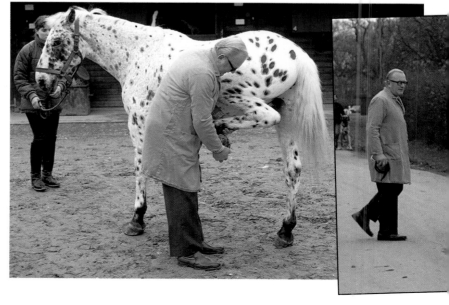

◄ **The vet** uses a rasp to level sharp edges. The long handle means the file can reach the back teeth. Most horses don't mind having their teeth rasped — once they get used to the odd noise!

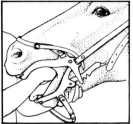

USING A GAG
Usually, a headcollar is enough to restrain the pony when the vet rasps the teeth.

Sometimes, however, he may insert a metal instrument known as a 'gag' into the horse's mouth to hold the jaws open. This helps him to get a better look at the back teeth. A 'gag' is also helpful for ponies that try to bite the rasp.

▼ **Routine health** procedures can get overlooked. Why not keep a calendar in the tack room, specially as a health planner for your pony?

(molars and premolars) should meet exactly, and should be worn evenly by the constant grinding action of the jaw.

In practice, the upper teeth usually lie slightly outside those in the lower jaw. This means that the inner edge of the upper teeth, and the outer edge of the lower teeth, tend to be worn more. The unworn outer edges of the upper teeth remain sharp and cut the cheeks, while the unworn inner edges of the lower teeth cut the tongue.

You must have your pony's teeth checked once a year to make sure that they are not sharp or worn irregularly. The vet can rasp off any sharp points and level the grinding surface of the teeth. This prevents a cut tongue or cheeks, and enables the pony to grind his food properly.

If he can't chew his food thoroughly, it passes through his system only partly digested or just drops out of his mouth. To absorb nutrients, your pony must be able to digest his food normally.

Old and young teeth

Young horses lose their temporary (milk) teeth between two and four years of age. The new permanent teeth can be sharp, and you may need to have them looked at more often – every six months – during this period.

Older horses, too, often have irregular teeth which don't meet properly. The teeth may have become loose, or even be missing. In this case, the tooth opposite the missing one is not worn down. It becomes long and sharp and may cut the pony's mouth. So more frequent attention is also required to keep older horses' teeth in good shape. Animals of this age (20 years and over) may need their teeth checked over at least twice a year.

Trotting the pony up

OCTOBER		Annual check up Vet 10 a.m.				
M		3	(10)	17	24	31
T		4	11	18	25	
W		5	12	19	26	
T		6	13	20	27	
F		(7)	14	21	28	
S	1	8	15	22	(29)	
S	2	9	16	23	30	

Farrier 11 a.m.   Worming

Worms and worming

▼ **Ponies at grass** must be wormed about every six weeks. You must dose ponies in the same field at the same time to have any effect. Be doubly sure to worm frequently in early and mid-summer, when the immature worms are most active.

Ask your vet how big a dose to give – and how often: the amount must be worked out by the pony's body weight and not by his height.

In the wild, horses graze over large areas and are rarely troubled by worms. Worms are a problem we have inflicted on horses by domesticating them and confining them to small areas of grazing. Regular worm treatment is probably the most important contribution you can make to keeping your pony healthy.

Why treat for worms?

The worms that live inside all horses are parasites – they feed off the tissues of other animals. Although it's difficult – if not impossible – to wipe out worm infection altogether, you can go a long way toward reducing the health problems that worms cause.

Treating your pony regularly (every six weeks) for worms has two benefits. You improve the horse's health by ridding him of harmful adult worms, and possibly immature worms (larvae) too (depending on which wormer you use). Equally important, you reduce the pasture contamination – lessening the risk of further infection to your pony and to others sharing the field.

Giving a worm medicine forms only part of a worm-control programme. Horses also have their own built-in worm defence mechanism – they are reluctant to eat grass near their drop-

pings (which contains most larvae).

Forcing them to do so, by over-grazing or keeping too many ponies on the same piece of ground, can have serious health consequences. Resting the grazing, picking up droppings at least once a week, and grazing with other farm stock (which eat horse worms but are not affected by them), all help reduce the risk to horses.

How to treat for worms

Worm treatments come in the form of powders or granules given in the food, or as pastes squirted into the horse's mouth. You can buy them from your vet or saddler.

You can give them yourself – there's no need to call the vet. Only in a few cases, where the horse is ill because of worm damage, may the vet have to give a more powerful drug, or larger doses of a suitable drug, by stomach tube.

Ponies are very clever at detecting 'doctored' food, so it's worth trying to disguise the taste of a wormer. Mix it with a small amount of bran mash, or add a sweetener like molasses. Most ponies also like bread. Sandwiching a powder between two slices often works.

Worm pastes, in a ready-loaded syringe, make sure the pony receives a full dose. Take trouble to give it properly, or the horse may spit it out.

★ **FIGURE PROBLEMS**
A moderately infected horse produces about *30 million* worm eggs a day! So an entire paddock can become seriously contaminated when grazed by one infected pony.

How to give a worm paste

1 If you are right handed, it is much easier to give the paste from the pony's right (off) side. If you're left handed, reverse the sides. Put a headcollar on your pony and ask a friend to stand by the left (near) shoulder and hold him. Make sure the pony has no food in his mouth.

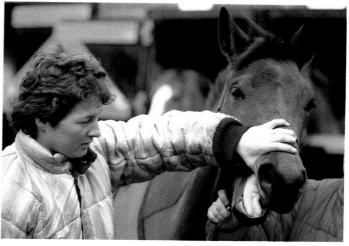

2 Hold the tube in your right hand. To open the pony's mouth, put your left hand on the bridge of his nose, just above the nostrils. Push your left thumb under the lip into the space behind the front teeth, and press the tip of your thumb against the roof of the mouth.

3 Keep your left hand in place and insert the tip of the tube to the back of the horse's mouth with your right hand. Squirt the contents on to the back of the tongue.

4 Withdraw the syringe quickly and close the mouth. Lift the pony's head in the air by holding a hand under his lower jaw. Wait until the pony swallows.

The different worms

There are many different varieties of worms that damage horses, and some are more serious than others. Most of them affect the digestive system, so the horse can't get enough nourishment to keep him healthy.

It's hard to identify which worms your horse is suffering from by his symptoms, so ask your vet which wormer he thinks is most suitable. The newer types kill worms at all stages of development.

Strongyloides attack the small intestine. They are only a problem in foals and yearlings and, in very young foals, may cause enteritis (inflamed intestines).

Roundworms, like strongyloides, mainly affect the small intestines of foals. They can have serious effects, including coughing and enteritis.

Bots are the larvae of the *Gastrophilus* fly. They affect the stomach and, in large numbers, can cause gastric ulcers.

Hairworms attack the stomach, resulting in a general loss of condition.

Pinworms (sometimes called seatworms) affect the large intestine. They irritate the rectum and the horse will seem to have an itchy tail.

Small redworms live in the large intestine and can cause severe disease. Grazing horses can pick up huge numbers of these parasites if not regularly wormed. The horse may have a pot belly, dull coat, anaemia, diarrhoea or colic.

Large redworms: Adult worms live in the large intestine, but the migrating larvae damage the horse's internal organs. Blood vessels supplying the bowels are most often affected. Large redworms are the commonest cause of colic.

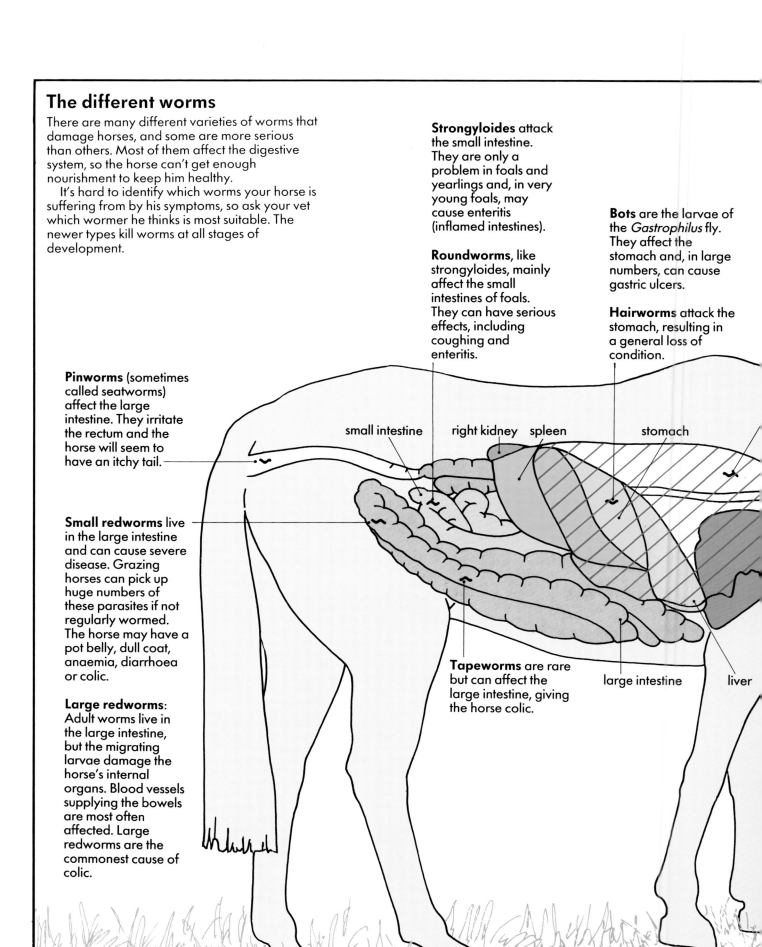

small intestine　　right kidney　　spleen　　stomach

Tapeworms are rare but can affect the large intestine, giving the horse colic.

large intestine　　liver

Life cycle of the large redworm

The large redworm (called in Latin *Strongylus vulgaris*) is the most damaging of all. Its total life cycle takes between eight and 11 months.

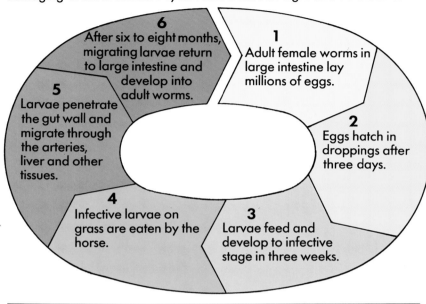

6 After six to eight months, migrating larvae return to large intestine and develop into adult worms.

5 Larvae penetrate the gut wall and migrate through the arteries, liver and other tissues.

1 Adult female worms in large intestine lay millions of eggs.

2 Eggs hatch in droppings after three days.

4 Infective larvae on grass are eaten by the horse.

3 Larvae feed and develop to infective stage in three weeks.

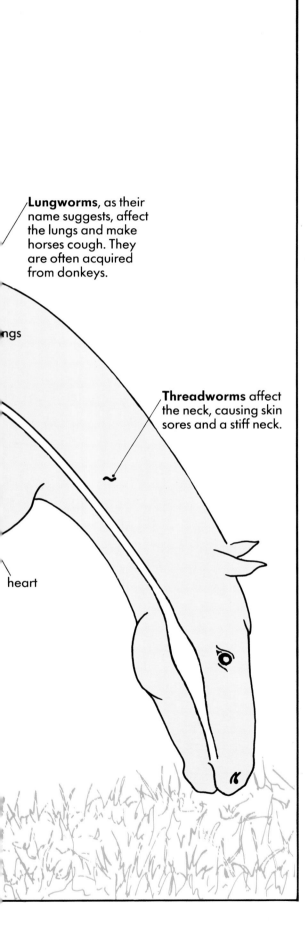

Lungworms, as their name suggests, affect the lungs and make horses cough. They are often acquired from donkeys.

ngs

Threadworms affect the neck, causing skin sores and a stiff neck.

heart

How horses are infected

Adult female worms living in the horse's intestines lay large numbers of eggs which are passed out in the droppings. In the warmth of the droppings, these eggs hatch to release tiny larvae which are too small to be seen with the naked eye. These move by wriggling, leaving the droppings to seek the moisture on the surface of the grass.

Within three to four weeks they develop into 'infective' larvae. These are swallowed by the horse. What then happens to the larvae depends on the species of worm. Some develop inside the wall of the bowel; others migrate through different organs.

Most adult horse worms live in the digestive system of their host, where they either suck blood, or live off digestive juices. The damage they do stops the horse being able to absorb nutrients from his food properly. Some worms penetrate the lining of the intestines, enter other internal organs and damage them. In large numbers, they can rupture the intestines.

Although horses acquire worms when they are grazing, the parasites can live inside the pony's body for several years and may not all be killed by worm treatment. Even horses that have been stabled for two or three years continually, with no access to grazing, may still have a few worms – in spite of being regularly treated.

WHAT THE LARGE REDWORM DOES

Large redworm larvae are particularly attracted to the blood vessels which supply the horse's bowels and intestines. The damage they cause in these vessels often severely affects the blood supply to the gut.

Over 90% of cases of colic are probably due to the effects of past or present infection with this particular parasite.

! WHEN TO WORM

If you have a new pony, worm him 24 hours before turning him out. A horse that is stabled through the winter should be wormed when he first comes in, and again when he goes out in the spring.

But if a pony is turned out to graze for part of the day, he will need worming at more frequent intervals — every six to eight weeks — even in winter.

179

Types of colic

To prevent colic – abdominal pain – you should worm regularly, feed top-quality food, and not let your pony become so hungry that he gorges himself. Colic, however, has a number of causes and, if you suspect your pony is suffering from this distressing condition, you should ring the vet immediately, whatever time of day or night.

Types of colic

Some types of colic are more serious than others but the symptoms are simi-lar – the pony looks fretfully at his sides, perhaps trying to bite at them. He paws the ground, maybe groaning, and patchy sweating breaks out. He rolls repeated-ly, but without shaking when he gets up (which ponies do when healthy). In very painful cases the pony may throw him-self around the box.

The first action the vet takes is to decide what might be the cause.

Spasmodic colic is the most common form. This is caused by a spasm (con-traction) of the bowel or by over-active movements of the bowel. If you give

▼ **Rolling** is generally a healthy sign. But a pony who keeps rolling, and doesn't shake himself when he gets up, may have colic – particularly if he shows other symptoms of distress.

unsuitable food, allow your horse to over-eat, or give cold water without taking the chill off it, this type of colic may develop.

Flatulent colic is due to a build up of gas in the bowel and is particularly common after eating foods which produce large amounts of gas by fermenting in the bowel. Too much of the wrong kinds of concentrates, particularly sugar beet pulp, may cause this kind of colic.

Impaction occurs when material which the horse cannot digest collects and blocks the bowel. It usually develops more slowly than other types of colic, often taking several days. Foods which have a very high content of woody material, or badly prepared foods containing sand or grit, may cause this condition.

Obstruction happens when the bowel becomes twisted on itself (called torsion or volvulus), telescopes into itself (intussusception), or something similar happens.

Obstruction may follow on from other types of colic, or from other diseases, or

► **Prevention** is much better than cure. Feed your pony little and often and make any changes in his diet *gradual*. An incorrect feeding regime is one of the major causes of colic.

▼ **A thirsty,** hot horse should be offered water with the chill taken off. Never work a horse hard immediately after he has had a long drink.

may develop by itself. This is a very serious type of colic and surgery is often necessary. In a few cases the damage to the bowel may be so great that surgery cannot save the horse.

Thromboembolism is one of the most complicated causes of colic. It is caused by worm larvae which have found their way into the blood vessels of the bowel. The larvae cause damage to the walls of the blood vessels, and blood clots develop which block the supply of blood. This results in severe damage to a section of bowel.

Treatment of this condition with drugs is often unsuccessful and the damage may well be too great for surgery to be possible. But prevention is easy – worm your pony regularly to ensure that this type of colic is very rare.

There are also cases of colic where no cause for the pain can be found.

Diagnosis and treatment

As soon as you have called the vet, think carefully about your horse's behaviour,

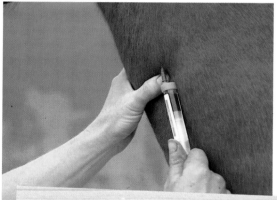

▲ **The vet** may listen to the horse's stomach to help him find the cause of colic.

► **Taking a blood** sample is another method the vet uses to make his diagnosis.

▲ **A tube** is passed down the nostril to the stomach. The vet uses it to put back fluids the horse may have lost through dehydration.

▼ **An injection** of antibiotics can speed up the horse's recovery.

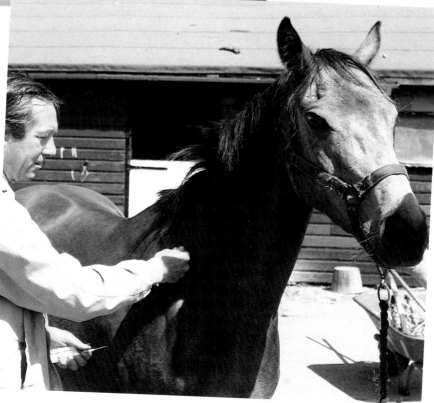

feeding and dunging over the last few days. The vet needs as much information as possible to help diagnosis.

He also examines the horse, maybe taking blood or fluid samples from the belly to find the answers. The vet may pass a tube down the nostril to the stomach, or examine the rectum.

The diagnosis depends to some extent on the response to the first stages of treatment. Early treatment usually consists of the vet injecting a pain killer either into the horse's muscles or directly into the bloodstream, using the jugular vein (the main vein in the neck). He may also give sedatives or antibiotics.

He uses the same methods to pass fluids into the body, as the horse may have become dehydrated. If the vet suspects impaction, he may also use a stomach tube to administer a laxative.

It is important that the vet can decide which sort of colic the pony has as soon as possible. If surgery is needed, the sooner the decision to operate on the pony is made, the better the chance of success.

All about laminitis

Laminitis is one of the commonest causes of lameness in ponies. The disease occurs when things go wrong within the structure of the hoof – and it's very painful.

What is laminitis?

Laminitis literally means an inflammation of the sensitive laminae within a horse's foot. The hoof becomes loosened from its attachment to the rest of the foot and, worse, the whole weight of the animal presses down on the sore area.

There is no human equivalent to laminitis, so it is hard for us to realize just how painful this disease is for a pony. However, think how sore a damaged fingernail can be when you knock it. Then imagine what it would be like if you had to support your bodyweight by balancing on sore fingernails!

What causes the disease?

Laminitis cannot be caught from other horses, and it rarely happens because of any foot problem. It develops because of toxins (poisons) released elsewhere in the horse's body which affect the circulation in its feet. There are several possible sources of toxins, but by far the most frequent is the bowels – where poisons originate because of feeding too much protein.

Many pony breeds have changed little over thousands of years. Their digestive systems evolved to deal with a sparse supply of a relatively coarse and indigestible material – grass. Ponies are not designed to cope with large amounts of lush protein-rich spring grass or concentrates.

Larger horses have been much more selectively bred by man, not only for their size, but to grow quickly and mature early. They can cope much better with a richer food supply.

So the commonest cause of laminitis is turning ponies out in lush grazing during late spring and early summer, particularly if the ground has been treated with fertilizer. Laminitis can strike at other times of the year, too, if you feed your pony too many rich concentrates for any length of time. It could also occur if your pony broke into the feed-store and gorged himself!

What are the signs?

Laminitis affects both front feet, and may well affect all four hooves. The pony is in severe pain and usually refuses to stand up or walk.

If he does stand, it is in a peculiar way – with his hindlegs well under his body to support its weight and with the front feet forward to leave as much weight on the heels as possible. When he has to move, it is with a pottering action, walking on his heels. The feet feel warm to the touch and the pony looks very sorry for himself.

He probably also has a temperature and a bounding pulse in the digital artery at the back of the pastern.

A pony who has had laminitis for a

long time is likely to have abnormal hooves – a 'dropped' sole from the bone pressing down, and laminitic rings because of differing hoof growth (a lot of heel growth and very little horn at the toe). The hoof wall may separate from the sole at the toe, with rotten horn in between – called 'seedy toe'.

Treating laminitis

You must call in the vet to treat the pony without delay, before foot changes go too far.

First, he will advise you to remove the cause of the trouble. This usually means taking the pony away from his grazing. It may also involve cutting out the concentrate ration, and feeding hay and water only.

Second, he will give a pain-killing injection as soon as possible. This works immediately, and he normally leaves more powders (to be given in the feed) to continue pain relief for several days.

Applying water from a hose or standing the feet in a running stream also helps, although hot water may be better to improve the circulation.

You need to relieve the pain so the animal can walk – which stimulates the

▼ **Horses** are much less likely to get laminitis than ponies because they have been carefully bred by humans and can cope with richer food.

circulation in the feet. The pain becomes less as the pony moves. About 10 minutes of leading at a walk, six times a day, should be enough.

Longer-term treatment

With long-term laminitis, you'll need both the vet and the farrier to correct hoof problems.

They have to remove any long or rotten horn at the toe to restore a more normal foot shape. Sometimes they have to cut away large amounts of the hoof wall at the front to allow healthy horn to grow down in its place.

The vet may take an X-ray to see how the foot can best be re-shaped. He may put on a special shoe to provide support and stop the bone moving downward.

Any horse that has suffered an attack of laminitis must be given a suitable vitamin, mineral and amino-acid feed supplement afterwards. This stimulates a good growth of new and healthy horn to replace the old, crumbling layers.

Preventing the disease

Ponies in general are prone to laminitis, and some individuals are highly susceptible. But in nearly every case, laminitis can be prevented with a little care and forethought.

This means never over-feeding your pony with concentrates. And don't let him on to lush grazing in early summer. If your pony gets fat on very little, be extra careful and try to keep his weight down. Laminitis is always worse in ponies that are overweight.

Some ponies may get laminitis even when on relatively poor grazing. In this case, you must remove the animal from grazing altogether during the summer months and just feed him on hay and water. Try to keep the pony in a large yard where he can move about, rather then confining him to a stable for long periods of time.

You must always be aware of the danger of laminitis and seek help the moment you notice any suspicious signs.

▲ **Hosing down** the legs can bring some relief to laminitis sufferers. However, some vets believe that warm water is better than cold because it improves the circulation.

Characteristic posture

A horse with a severe attack of laminitis appears rooted to the spot and is unwilling to move. The hindfeet are tucked under the body to take the weight off the forelegs. The forelegs are extended forward to keep the weight on the heels.

The condition is very painful and the horse may appear to be in distress.

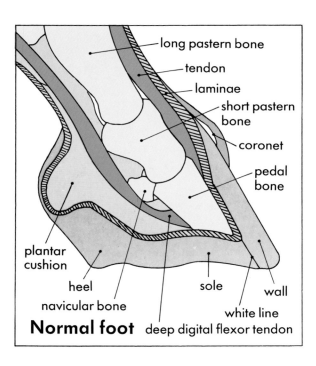

long pastern bone
tendon
laminae
short pastern bone
coronet
pedal bone

plantar cushion
heel
sole
wall
navicular bone
white line
Normal foot deep digital flexor tendon

Golden rules – laminitis do's and don'ts

DO always look for signs of laminitis when you check your horse each day. If he is reluctant to get up or move, feel his front feet for signs of heat.

DO call the vet without delay if you suspect your pony may be developing laminitis.

DO be extra careful if you know your pony has ever had laminitis before. He is likely to get it again.

DO be sure to bolt the feed-store door so that it is impossible for a pony to break in and gorge himself.

DO get a farrier to attend to your pony's feet regularly and keep shoes on him all the time if he suffers from chronic laminitis.

DO ask your vet to recommend a suitable mineral, vitamin and amino-acid feed supplement if your pony has hoof problems from chronic laminitis, or has recently sufffered an attack. The supplement stimulates new growth of healthy hoof horn.

DON'T turn ponies out into lush grazing in spring and early summer.

DON'T treat grazing used by ponies with nitrogen fertilizers.

DON'T let your pony get fat. Laminitis is always more of a problem in overweight horses.

DON'T over-feed your pony on concentrates at any time of the year.

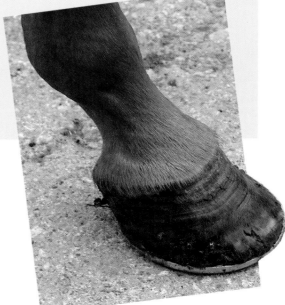

▲ **Signs** of laminitis are long toes, flat soles and worn heels. Because the toes have little wear, the horn there hardly grows at all, while the heels keep producing it. This unevenness causes 'rings' around the hoof wall.

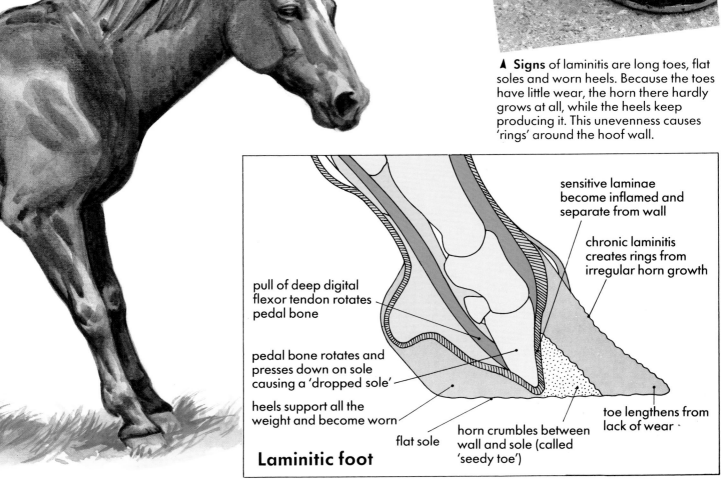

sensitive laminae become inflamed and separate from wall

chronic laminitis creates rings from irregular horn growth

pull of deep digital flexor tendon rotates pedal bone

pedal bone rotates and presses down on sole causing a 'dropped sole'

heels support all the weight and become worn

flat sole

horn crumbles between wall and sole (called 'seedy toe')

toe lengthens from lack of wear

Laminitic foot

Strains and splints

Pushing your horse on over stony ground, and particularly down hills, can be a cause of strains. Always make sure your horse is properly warmed up before strenuous exercise.

As a horse is an athlete, injury to the legs is very common. Working a pony too hard when he is not properly fit can lead to problems and lameness.

The tendons

Strains happen when the horse's movement is at its most strenuous. If you make a horse gallop when he is unfit or force him on in heavy going, or when he's tired, the muscles can no longer use their elasticity to cushion the shock.

The shock is then thrown upon the tendons. As these have very little elasticity – unlike the rubbery muscles – they strain or even rupture. The foreleg muscles take the most weight and are more quickly fatigued than the larger ones in the hindlegs, so strains occur most frequently in the front legs.

They are also more likely to affect the *flexor* tendons which are responsible for lifting the leg off the ground. The *extensor* tendons carry the leg forward after it has left the ground. They have less work to do and so take less strain.

The best way to prevent your horse from straining his legs is never to gallop him when he's unfit, and never to push him on when he is tired.

Treating a strain

Once a tendon has become stretched beyond its limit – strained – the horse is usually lame with considerable swelling and pain if you press the area. In severe cases the back tendon area 'bows' outward. Call the vet as surgical treatment may be necessary.

Luckily, lameness because of tendon trouble is not usually so severe – the severity depends on the number of fibres ruptured. But even with mild strains, rest the horse in a stable, bandage the leg and call the vet.

The ligaments

Strains can occur to the ligaments. Ligaments hold the bones together and are made of fibres like tendons, but they are even less elastic.

Shock from fast work on hard ground or general overwork in an old horse can produce strains. If the horse slips and the legs splay outward at an unnatural angle this may well wrench a ligament.

Try *not* to work your horse at swift paces on hard, stony surfaces. As he gets older, reduce his jumping work.

▲ **Racehorses** are prone to leg injuries, and working over heavy going doesn't help. To cut down the risk of strains and splints, they are trained gradually to a peak of fitness – like all athletes.

 **STRAIN OR SPRAIN?** You may hear the word 'sprain' used instead of 'strain'. Strictly speaking, however, a strain describes *stretching* which causes injury, while a sprain describes an injury caused by a *knock or compression.*

► Jumping, particularly landing, puts great stress on the horse's forelegs.

▲ **If you suspect** your horse is lame, call the vet. He will diagnose the cause by feeling the legs for swelling, splints or other problems.

Tendons and muscles

The tendons connect the muscles to the bones in the leg. Imagine the muscles in the upper leg as large rubber straps and the tendons below them as wires.

When the muscles contract, they pull the tendon 'wires' up. As these are attached to the bones in the hoof, the foot is pulled off the ground and forward.

But, if the 'wiry' tendons are over-stretched, they become strained — the fibres tear apart.

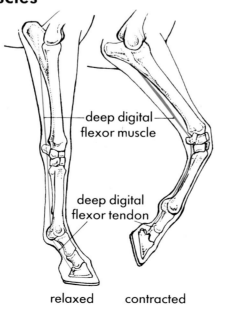

deep digital flexor muscle

deep digital flexor tendon

relaxed   contracted

Resting

All 'cures' depend on helping the body's natural mechanism for repair of damaged tissue. Rest is the most important factor in healing any injury. It lets the body right itself naturally. However, most horses need gentle exercise after a few days — walking for short periods several times a day — to pump away unwanted fluid from the injury. Ask your vet for advice.

After the pain and swelling have gone down, you can turn the horse out into a small, level paddock where he cannot gallop about. Do not return him to hard work too soon but bring him back to fitness in easy stages. Strains can take up to 18 months to heal.

Splints

A splint is a layman's term for a firm swelling found on the splint bone where it connects to the cannon bone. Splints mostly occur in the foreleg – you can feel a hard lump on the inside of the leg. If they occur in the hindleg, they are generally on the *outside*.

There are two splint bones: one on either side of the cannon bone in each leg. They are held to the cannon bone by ligaments. In young horses these ligaments may become inflamed.

After the age of four the splint bones are fused to the cannon bone. Splints occur as a result of concussion (shock), for example, when an immature horse is given excessive work on hard ground. Faulty shoeing can also be a factor as it throws an uneven strain on the leg.

The swelling can be any size. The horse may or may not be lame, depending on the position of the swelling and the extent of the injury.

When they are forming, splints feel spongy with some heat and are painful when pressed. To examine for splints, lift the leg and run your finger and thumb along the groove at the back of the cannon. Do not mistake the nodules at the lower end for splints as there are natural 'buttons' at the bottom of the splint bone.

Rest and reduced work is all that is generally needed with a young animal. With a mature horse, splints that feel cool and are not high up do not cause lameness and don't much matter. Call the vet to make sure there is not a fracture of the splint bone.

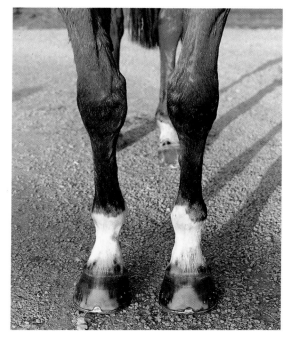

How to tell if a horse is lame

Most lameness occurs below the knee of the foreleg and from the hock down in the hindleg. A lame horse is one that does not move freely, or moves with an unnatural gait. He may step 'short' at the walk, so that the front legs look as if they are pottering. Or the hindlegs may not 'track up' – one doesn't reach as far forward as its opposite number.

At the trot, a lame horse 'drops' on one side and throws up his head as the lame front leg comes to the ground. If it is a hindleg that is lame, the quarters are carried higher on one side.

◄ **Splints** are hard swellings caused by overwork on hard ground. They do not necessarily cause lameness.

❗ RACEHORSE WARNING

'Breakdowns' in the lower legs of young racehorses are fairly common. This is partly due to the fact that these horses are made to work too hard for their immature physique.

If you have any part in the care of a horse under the age of four or five, take care to bring him on slowly. Have the vet check that the joints, ligaments and tendons can stand up to it before you ask the horse to perform really strenuous work. Then he will have much less trouble from sprains and splints.

◄ **Rest cures:** Horses recovering from lameness should be confined to a small paddock so that they cannot gallop about.

Treating cuts and bruises

One of the reasons for checking a pony at least once a day is to look for wounds. Even small cuts need treatment and, if you find one, you should apply first aid.

Types of wounds

How you reduce risk of injury and treat a horse wound depends on what type it is.

Clean-cut (incised) wounds are straight edged. They are usually clean with no surrounding tissue damage or bruising. However, they may cut into joints such as tendons and so can be serious. Make sure you clear sharp objects like glass from the box, yard or paddock. When setting up practice fences, check the ground around them as the pony is most likely to fall while jumping.

Torn (lacerated) wounds: The skin is torn apart, leaving irregular edges. The muscles underneath may be damaged or torn, depending on where your pony is

▼ **Cross-country jumps:** Protect the pony's legs in case he hits one of the fences. Check him over carefully afterwards for cuts, bruises or splinters of wood.

wounded and how fast he or the object was travelling at the time.

Barbed wire is the most likely cause. A startled pony can run into the fence and the wire tangles around his legs. As the pony pulls the wire tightens, and the barbs tear the flesh, causing deep and serious wounds. Any type of wire fence can be dangerous, so use wooden railing if possible.

Puncture wounds are caused by an object like a nail driving through the skin and passing into the body. They can be very misleading. A tiny wound can look like nothing but, if caused by a fork prong, there may be a lot of damage under the skin. Worse, a wooden object could leave splinters inside the wound. Always mend broken fencing immediately. Never take your pony through a narrow gap where twigs or other pointed objects protrude. Put your fork away safely – don't leave it lying around the yard.

Bruised wounds (contusions): The force of the blow breaks the skin and bruises the tissue underneath, causing swelling under the skin. The legs are most commonly affected – the pony may bruise himself by overreaching or brushing, or by kicking a jump or crashing over it. Boots or exercise bandages help protect the pony's legs while jumping.

Treatment

Wounds are usually quite easy to see, except for small punctures. Always check your pony every day so you are familiar with how he looks and feels normally. Then, when a small wound occurs, you notice the swelling or small patch of blood. Finding the wound early means you can treat it promptly and the pony recovers quickly.

First you must stop the bleeding. Press firmly on the wound with a clean cloth or wad of cotton wool. If the wound is on the leg, wrap a crêpe bandage fairly tightly over the cotton wool to keep the pressure on. You can apply a simple circular bandage to most areas but a figure-of-eight bandage over fetlock, knee and hock joints gives better contact. If you can't stop the bleeding, call the vet.

Once the bleeding has stopped, the wound needs a good wash with antiseptic and water. Remove all the grit and mud, but try not to disturb the clots as the wound may start bleeding again. A clean-cut wound with little bruising or complications is best left uncovered. The dry air helps form a clean scar quickly, and the cut heals rapidly.

However, all lower leg wounds should be bandaged to prevent further contami-

► **Exercise bandages,** which run from just below the hocks or knees to just above the fetlocks, guard the legs from jumping injuries.

BEWARE!

▲ **Glass:** Sharp edges cause 'clean-cut' wounds which can be severe if on a joint. Broken glass may be left inside the wound and is hard to see.

▲ **Wire** can cause tear wounds if the pony panics and gets tangled up in it. Barbed wire is most dangerous.

▲ **Sharp prongs** puncture the skin, leaving deep wounds that can result in serious infection. Never leave pitchforks lying around.

HOCKS AND KNEES
Normally if your pony has a cut or graze which needs bandaging, you can put on a crêpe or self-adhesive bandage over a non-stick dressing. But with hocks, knees and fetlocks, the bandage has to be flexible enough to let the pony move.

You can either buy special contour bandages, which are stretchy and fasten with zips, or put on an exercise bandage in the shape of a figure of eight.

▲ **Get expert help** especially with lower leg wounds which must always be bandaged.

nation. And any wound that is getting dirty should be covered with a piece of Melolin or paraffin gauze under a bandage. Change the bandage daily and check for weeping from the wound. If yellow discharges of pus, excessive swelling or lameness appear call the vet before they get worse.

Large clean-cut and torn wounds may need stitching to repair the damaged tissue underneath. Puncture wounds and large ones are best treated with antibiotic, both topically (on the wound) and systemically (injected). Bruised wounds, particularly if they are very swollen, need cold compresses to stop haemorrhage for the first hour. Then Lasonil ointment should be applied.

Finally, don't panic. If you are unsure of what to do, call the vet.

Putting on a figure-of-eight bandage

1 Cut gamgee to fit the area around the hock and place it around the leg — not too tightly or you restrict the pony's movement. Wrap the bandage round once above the hock.

2 Pass the bandage down in a diagonal round the front of the hock, and wrap it round the leg. Do another diagonal turn to above the hock and repeat until secure.

3 When you reach the end of the bandage, pull the tapes apart so that they are straight and flat. Wind them round the leg and tie them on the outside in a bow.

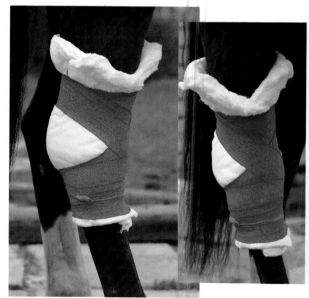

4 Tuck the tapes in so they don't get in the way. There should be no pressure on any part of the joint and no bandage around the point of the hock or the pony can't move.

The medicine chest

It is essential for all horse owners to have at least a basic first-aid kit in case of accidents and emergencies.

Most items are readily available from good chemists. Otherwise your vet can advise you on what to buy and where to get it from.

The basic kit

The first thing you need is a container. Use a clean box, cupboard or drawer for storing the first-aid items. Keep it in the house or tack room. A portable box or strong bag is also useful for taking a kit to shows. Your medicine chest should contain the following:

A mild antiseptic solution for bathing wounds.

Antiseptic or antibiotic cream to ward off infection.

Moist pads for cleaning wounds, when clean water is not available.

Melolin non-adhesive dressing pads.

A small clean bucket kept only for bathing wounds.

Some kind of poultice dressing such as 'Animalintex'. A poultice is applied to a wound either to draw 'poison' from an abscess, or to reduce swelling – on a sprained tendon for example. Another

product that you can use for this purpose is Kaolin.

Gamgee tissue for bathing wounds and for padding and protecting them under bandages. Gamgee is cotton wool covered with gauze to stop 'fluff' sticking to wounds.

Clean elasticated bandages for keeping dressings in place. Crêpe exercise bandages are effective. Keep two clean ones in your kit. Non-stretch gauze bandages are little use as they nearly always come off, while stretchy ones mould to the leg and stay on better.

A pair of curved scissors for cutting dressings.

Optrex for bathing eyes.

A clinical thermometer to take a horse's temperature.

Maintaining your kit

It is important to keep the container clean. A dirty container is unhygienic. Also, keep equipment like scissors clean. Always wipe and replace tops of bottles, tubes and jars after use.

Keep gamgee and other dressings well wrapped up and wash bandages in hot, soapy water after each use. Rinse them in clear water containing a little antiseptic liquid.

First-aid kits should be on hand when needed and contain all their basic items. When you start getting low on a particular item, put it on a special list and get the replacement *before* you run out.

Keep a permanent list of what should be in the kit and check it regularly. If any item has run out you can then replace it in plenty of time.

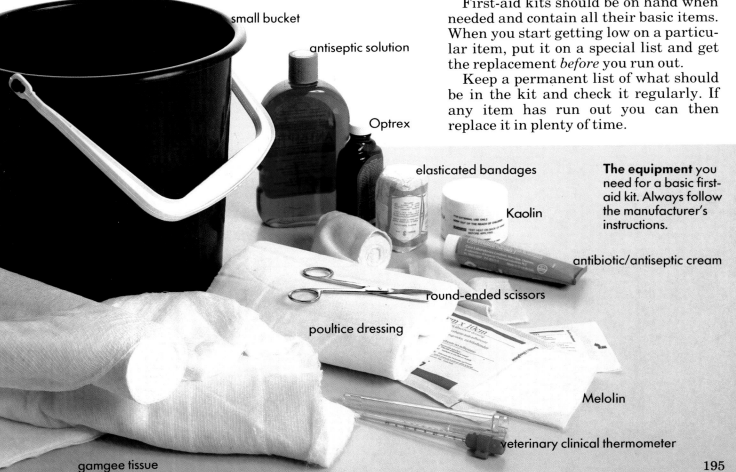

small bucket

antiseptic solution

Optrex

elasticated bandages

Kaolin

The equipment you need for a basic first-aid kit. Always follow the manufacturer's instructions.

antibiotic/antiseptic cream

round-ended scissors

poultice dressing

Melolin

veterinary clinical thermometer

gamgee tissue

Looking after a foal: 1

A foal of your own! It's an appealing idea for anybody – especially if you have a favourite mare as the prospective mother. But, while the basics of foal care are worth learning, the best advice for the novice owner is to follow expert advice.

Think things through

Even with an experienced horse breeder in charge, things can go wrong. The mare may have difficulties during foaling, her youngster may be born with a weakness or disability or could even have an accident while in the paddock.

It's important to think about these unpleasant possibilities beforehand. More important, though, you must think about the young foal's growing years and plan five, six or 10 years ahead.

You may want to keep your youngster. But suppose he grows up to have a bad fault of conformation or a difficult temperament? Or what if he is too small – or big – for you to ride?

Then again, your lifestyle could change. You might not be able to keep horses or might find it difficult to feed and look after both a mare and her

▼ **At grass:** Foals can be turned out with their mothers or with other youngsters. Make sure the field is well fenced and contains no hazardous wire or litter.

rapidly growing young foal.

Even if you plan to sell the foal, you must be prepared to care for him until he is old enough to be backed and schooled for riding. Trying to take short cuts by selling too soon is potentially fatal for the youngster: few new owners want to take on an unproven foal and the most likely buyer could be someone from a local slaughterhouse.

Pony buyers

Pony buyers today can be choosers. For a foal to have any chance of finding a good, lasting home, he should be *out of* (have as his mother) a pony whose own conformation, performance record and temperament are well above average. For preference, the mare should have the prizes to prove it – from good-class shows, trials or other competitions.

The stallion should be selected to produce a good foal from your particular mare, countering in his conformation any flaws in her shape. The foal must also be *well done* (fed and looked after) and well handled by knowledgeable people throughout his babyhood and young life so that he does not acquire any bad habits.

▼ **A young foal** may be adorable but he grows up! Breeding is a responsible job and should only be undertaken by experts.

Looking after a foal: 2

As well as getting a foal used to human handling, breeding from a mare means you are responsible for the health of mother and baby.

The newborn foal

Most foals are born at night, and mares prefer to deal with the birth in peace, though a watchful eye should be kept on them. The birth is near when the mare's udder swells, wax shows on her teats, and the muscles around the root of her tail relax as her body prepares for the foal to be born.

A pony mare may foal out of doors – as she would in the wild – but this has dangers in a small, crowded paddock, where she cannot escape from other horses to have her foal in peace. A refined breed of mare, on a stud, is brought into a special foaling box.

A normal birth comes front feet first. The foal 'dives' out into the world and, in the process, breaks the protective membrane surrounding it. After the foal is born, the mare also delivers the afterbirth (placenta), in which the foal has grown in her womb. This usually comes away cleanly within an hour or so. If the afterbirth, or parts of it, remain inside the mare, this could cause blood poisoning and very acute laminitis. The vet must be called in quickly because this is an emergency.

▼ **After a healthy birth,** this Dartmoor mare and her one-day old foal are soon out at grass. While its mother enjoys her grazing, the foal takes a first bewildering glimpse at the outside world.

After a normal birth, mare and foal are soon on their feet. The mare licks and nudges the foal, cleaning and warming it. Humans may long to help as the foal totters about seeking the mare's udder (often between her forelegs, first try!) but mother and baby are best left on their own to tackle this early problem naturally.

A foal's vital first feed is not ordinary milk but a rich substance called colostrum. This helps the foal resist disease and pass the hard black dung accumulated in his gut while in the womb; the digestive system can then work normally. It is critical that the foal receives his colostrum.

▲ Newly born: The mother nudges the foal and licks its coat to clean and warm it up. The foal should be on its feet and trying to suckle within the first two hours of its life.

★ TIMING DEVICE
Racehorse breeders like mares to 'foal down' as near January 1 as possible. This is the official birthday of all Thoroughbreds. A colt born at the natural time, around midsummer, would be only 18 months old when asked to compete in two-year-old races, a big disadvantage.

► **Suckling** is the foal's main source of food for the first four to six months of its life. When it reaches this age, it should be gradually weaned away from its mother.

Weaning

Weaning means separating a foal from its mother, both to set the youngster on its way to becoming an adult, independent horse, and to stop the drain on the mare of feeding her fast-growing colt or filly. The foal will have been given solid food well before it is weaned, to avoid too much shock to its system. Afterwards, it needs a high protein diet to build its strength during the vital years of fast growth to four years old. A youngster stunted and starved in the 'weanling' stage seldom recovers fully.

Foals are ready for weaning at four to six months old. Exactly when depends on their date of birth. Pony mares are generally best covered (mated) so they foal down – about 11 months later – at the natural season in early summer. It is warm, there is plenty of grass, and the foal has every chance to thrive.

Weaning involves taking the mare out of earshot of her foal. The foal may be left behind in the stable one morning when the mare goes out to the paddock. It helps if the foal can see another youngster next door. Alternatively, if several mares and foals share a paddock, the mare may be taken out while the foal stays with its friends. Either way, youngsters – and their mothers – soon settle, given good food and good handling, plus another pony for company.

Medical matters

In-foal mares, like all ponies, need regular worming. A worm dose a month before the mare is due to foal reduces the risk of her newborn foal picking up worms from his dam's droppings. The newly weaned youngster also needs worming.

All horses should be injected against

▼ **Tetanus vaccinations** are essential. A course of injections for the first 15 months protects a foal from this horrible disease.

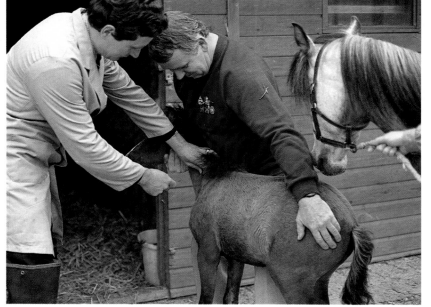

▼ **By the time** they are yearlings, most colt foals have been gelded (neutered). Allowed to recover at grass, geldings are much calmer and easier to manage than stallions.

tetanus, a horrible and usually fatal disease. An in-foal mare given a 'booster tetanus jab' a month before foaling passes on protection to her foal in the colostrum – vital, since foals are careless of their own safety! A course of injections over its first 15 months should then give the young pony protection.

Colt foals, except those to be kept for breeding, must also be gelded (neutered). The testicles are surgically removed, under anaesthetic. This can be done when the youngster is a foal, provided he is strong and well grown, and that the testicles have both 'come down' from inside his body into the skin bag that holds them (the scrotum). Alternatively, gelding can be left until he is a yearling.

Usually, the operation is carried out in either autumn or spring, when flies are not a bother but the weather is fine enough to let the newly gelded pony out for plenty of exercise, to work off any swelling.

He soon recovers, and his quieter ways as a gelding are a relief both to any mares he has been trying to woo, and to the humans who are handling him! Entire (ungelded) colts can become difficult to manage from as young as nine or 10 months old – one more reason why owning a foal is not for the novice!

Looking after an old horse

▼ **Having an old horse** in your care is a rewarding responsibility. Look after him well and he'll repay you with years of faithful service.

The care of an old horse depends upon his condition and circumstances rather than on his actual age. While horses in heavy work are usually retired between the ages of 12 and 15, a gently used pony can continue to lead an active life well into his 20s.

At grass

The work required of an older pony should be less frequent and not too vigorous, so it is usually best to keep him at grass where he can take his own exercise. If he has always been stabled in the past, let him get used to life outside gradually.

Even more than most, old horses appreciate the protection of good thick hedges or an open shed in the field. Bring your pony in at night during the colder months. Put him in a New Zealand rug if he's newly turned out in bad weather or if he has not yet re-grown a full coat after clipping.

One of the values of an old horse is as a calming friend to a younger, excitable pony. All horses, being herd animals, are naturally happier in company. But watch out that your old pony is not bullied by a number of younger animals – you have to separate them if this happens.

Feeding

To maintain his body heat and condition, an older pony needs more food than a middle-aged one. But the proportion of concentrated to bulk food (hay and grass) changes. Carry out any adjustments in diet gradually. The total quantity of food needed each day by a 14-hand pony is about 9kg (20lbs) and for a horse doing no work this can be entirely bulk. But, to build up condition in a neglected older animal or for one carrying out a modest amount of work, give a proportion of concentrates.

If the pony is still being gently ridden by young riders, pony nuts or cubes are most suitable. Barley adds variety to the food and helps to condition an old horse in poor shape without exciting him.

If your pony is at grass, fresh water, grass and hay should ideally be unlimited because most ponies adjust their intake to their needs. The only time to restrict grazing is when the pony is first turned out on to lush spring paddocks, fertilized pastures or clover fields.

Exercise

Daily exercise is essential for the horse at any age. While an older, grass-kept pony can exercise himself, even an old, sick horse benefits from being led out for half an hour. And a stabled pony who is fairly fit can cope with an hour or more of gentle hacking including modest jumping, a canter and hillwork.

However, galloping about at gymkhanas, hunting or eventing is unsuitable. Whatever is asked of an old pony should be built up slowly and in ▶

▼ **At grass:** Old ponies are often most content in a field. The hollow back is a typical sign of ageing and does not interfere with the pony's ability to exercise himself.

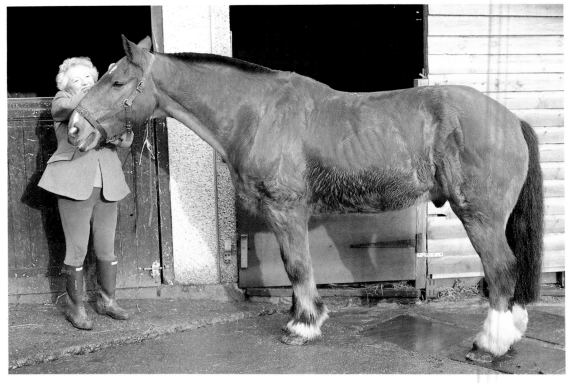

► **Take particular care** to check an old horse every day for wounds, lameness, coughing and skin problems.

▼ ► **Exercise:** Even if your horse isn't up to being ridden, lead him round lanes or through fields to stop him getting stiff.

A daily half-hour 'walk' is especially important if he's kept in a stable.

keeping with his former capabilities.

Health problems

You must take extra care to keep to all the routines of good horse management with an older animal. The daily check for problems is particularly important.

Teeth should be filed at least once a year. The outer edges of the upper molars and the inner edges of the lower molars get less wear and become very sharp. This can cause an old pony to refuse food and fight shy of the bit. He may even get attacks of colic (bad stomach ache) from poor chewing.

Feet: The pony only needs to be shod if he is doing roadwork. But even unshod, his feet must be regularly checked and filed to keep the soles level, and trimmed to prevent hooves splitting.

Brushing (striking the inner side of the opposite leg) can be the result of age or overwork. Protective boots are available and the blacksmith can help with special shoeing techniques.

Ponies frequently rest a hindleg on the tip of the hoof. But if this 'pointing' occurs with a front leg it is usually a sign of trouble. There are many causes of lameness in the older pony and you should always seek your vet's advice.

Coughs and colds: Old ponies catch coughs and colds readily. They can have chest problems which cause breathing difficulties. Provide rest and extra warmth and call the vet if you're not sure what to do.

Lumps, bumps and tumours frequently appear on old ponies. Although unsightly, they may be harmless – but leave that decision to the vet.

Worming: Do this at least every three months, especially for an old pony in a field used by a number of other horses. Worms are often the reason for a pony's condition failing to improve and for his harsh, staring coat.

Skin problems like mange, ringworm, lice, ticks and warts tend to arise more often on the older horse. All are curable with the correct treatment, so ask your vet. Remember to separate a pony with a skin disease or problem from other horses, as some are catching.

This may seem like a long list of ailments but, provided you cultivate a good local vet and are methodical with the daily check, most problems can be nipped in the bud.

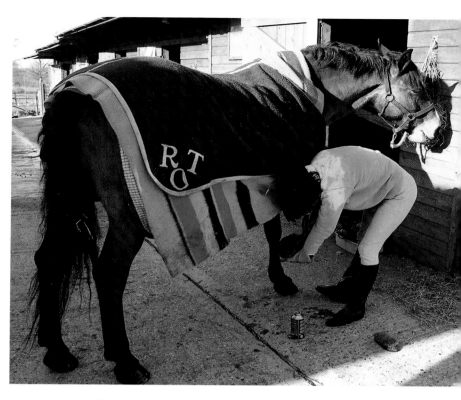

▲ **Keeping warm:** The sun may be shining, but the chill of winter quickly penetrates old horses' bones. A horse that's tied up can't move around to keep warm, so make sure he has plenty of rugs on while you attend to stable chores.

◄ **Young riders** and old horses are an excellent match: mature ponies are tolerant and kind to novices going through their paces. This pony is 28 years old and still giving hours of pleasure.

Index

ACKNOWLEDGEMENTS

Photographers: A.G.E. Fotostock 40, 43(t); Animal
Photography 47(t), 184–5, (R. Wilbie) 26(tr), 43(c);
Aquila Photographics (R. Maier) 26(bl), 36, 45(c), 47(b),
120(c), 180–1, (J.F. Preedy) 35(b); Simon Butcher/
Eaglemoss 195; Bruce Coleman/Eric Crichton 75(t);
Robert Estall 24(c); Mary Evans Picture Library 12;
Harry Hall 58; Robert Harding Picture Library 73(b); Kit
Houghton 6–7, 31, 33, 34(b), 37, 45(t,b), 56–57,
87(inset), 110–111, 138, 151, 182(t), 186(t),
197(inset), 199(t); Kit Houghton/Eaglemoss 52–53, 55;
Bob Langrish 27(t), 29(t), 43(b), 47(c), 49(b), 68, 70(b),
139, 150, 164(t), 165(c), 166–167, 169(b), 172–173,
174, 175(t,b), 182(b), 183(t,c), 187(t), 188–190, 190(l),
191(t); Lavenham Rugs 54(cr), 122(cl); National Motor
Museum 19; NHPA (B. Chaumeton) 35(tr), (P. Fagot)
35(tl); Octopus Books (C. Linton) 72; Nick Rains/
Eaglemoss 194(bl); Mike Roberts 82(t), 120(t), 200(t),
201(b); Peter Roberts Collection 74, 82(c,b), 84(cl), 89,
122(bl), 168(l), 183(b); The Slide File 25(br); Sporting
Pictures 190(t); Tony Stone Worldwide 2–3, 42, 46;
John Suett/Projekt Photography/Eaglemoss 29(b),
75(b), 107(b), 126, 130, 136(l), 143; Survival Anglia
Picture Library (L&T Bomford) 28(b); Shona Wood/
Eaglemoss front cover, 4–5, 24(bl,r), 25(t,c), 28(t), 48,
49(t,c), 50–51, 54(b), 57(inset), 60–64, 66–67, 69,
70(t), 71, 73(inset), 76–83, 84(cr,b), 85–87, 88(tc),
90–92, 94–106, 107(t), 108–109, 112–119, 120(b),
121, 122(tc,br), 123–125, 128–129, 131–134, 136–
137, 140–149, 152–163, 164(b), 165(b), 168(br,cr),
169(tr,tc), 170–171, 175(br), 176–177, 191(b), 192–
193, 194(t,br), 196–197, 200(b), 201(t), 202–205;
Zefa Picture Library 27(b), 44, 198–199, (R. Sponlein)
34(t).

Illustrators: Catherine Constable 18–23, 30, 32–33,
178–179, 186–187; Michael Cooke/Eaglemoss 81,
108, 130, 139; Denys Ovenden 31, 81, 113(r), 127,
140–141, 193; Maggie Raynor 8–11, 13–17, 24–25,
37–39, 41, 59, 63, 65, 93, 113(t), 135, 160–161,
163–164, 190.